FAMILY REFERENCE

BECOMING A FATHER

How to make a success of
your role as a parent

Mike Lilley

How To Books

By the same author
Successful Single Parenting

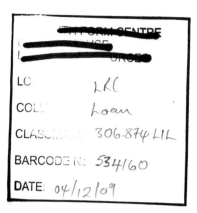

Cartoons by Mike Flanagan

British Library Cataloguing in Publication Data
A catalogue record for this book is available from the British Library.

First published in 1997 by How To Books Ltd, 3 Newtec Place,
Magdalen Road, Oxford, OX4 1RE, United Kingdom.
Tel: (01865) 793806. Fax: (01865) 248780.

Note: The material contained in this book is set out in good faith for
general guidance and no liability can be accepted for loss or expense
incurred as a result of relying in particular circumstances on statements
made in the book. The laws and regulations are complex and liable to
change, and readers should check the current position with the relevant
authorities before making personal arrangements.

Produced for How To Books by Deer Park Productions.
Typeset by PDQ Typesetting, Stoke-on-Trent, Staffs.
Printed and bound by Cromwell Press, Broughton Gifford, Melksham,
Wiltshire.

BECOMING A FATHER

A selection of Family Reference titles in this Series

Applying for Legal Aid
Arranging Insurance
Be a Local Councillor
Be an Effective School Governor
Becoming a Father
Buying a Personal Computer
Cash from Your Computer
Choose a Private School
Choosing a Nursing Home
Choosing a Package Holiday
Claim State Benefits
Dealing with a Death in the Family
Helping Your Child to Read
Lose Weight & Keep Fit

Make a Wedding Speech
Making a Complaint
Managing Your Personal Finances
Plan a Wedding
Prepare Your Child for School
Raise Funds & Sponsorship
Run a Local Campaign
Run a Voluntary Group
Successful Grandparenting
Successful Single Parenting
Survive Divorce
Take Care of Your Heart
Taking In Students

Other titles in preparation

The How To series now contains more than 200 titles in the following categories:

Business Basics
Family Reference
Jobs & Careers
Living & Working Abroad
Student Handbooks
Successful Writing

Please send for a free copy of the latest catalogue for full details (see back cover for address).

Contents

Preface

This book is written with an important principle in mind, that although men cannot physically have babies and cannot breastfeed, they as fathers can do everything else. In a modern society where traditional divisions between gender roles are breaking down it is important to give our children a view that nothing is beyond them nor beneath them. For example, a girl can be an astronaut and a boy can remain at home and care for his children – both jobs are valuable and equal. Children do benefit from the involvement of two parents, and two parents are preferable to finance a growing family, but single parents can successfully rear children and children can be reared successfully by fathers on their own.

The principle of the father's importance as a valuable parent does not go away just because the family structure changes. Quality of parenting is more important than quantity. Research into fathers after divorce found that a number who had been the traditional breadwinner and 'night fathers', when suddenly faced with fighting for custody and access of their children had for the first time to really consider their role as father. They had to plan access weekends carefully, and found that they ended up having more quality time with their children than before the divorce. It often takes the thought or act of losing to make us realise the real value of what we had. Children do need to be financed but they are not a commodity in themselves: they are flesh and blood, and they need your time and love far more than money.

Fatherhood is a very misunderstood term, usually defined purely on the basis of our personal experiences of our own fathers. My father never knew his father, except briefly as an adult, and he wanted his children's experience to be different. He was someone I deeply respected and wanted to know, but I nevertheless felt he was far away and removed. As far as I can remember, he never kissed or gave me a cuddle. His role was to be the financial provider, the man who gave us a roof over our heads. I wanted to hold my kids, be there for them, have strong physical contact, a contact I had longed for with my own father. We do learn from our parents, even if it is the strong view of wanting our children to be brought up differently.

Bookshop shelves are full of titles dealing with motherhood. The few books concerned with fatherhood concentrate on the birth years or divorce. My aim has been to write a fathers' manual which provides an overview of what is involved in becoming a father of children from birth and beyond, whether through a continuing relationship or through divorce.

The book is based on the real-life experiences of many fathers. However, the case studies which illustrate the text use fictional characters and situations, and any resemblance to living persons is entirely coincidental.

Michael Lilley

Father should become:

- capable of change

- good at managing change

- open and fair minded

- responsible

- flexible

- able to cope

- close to his children

- supportive and co-operative

- involved

- able to learn

- tolerant

- able to listen

- firm and fair

Fatherhood involves:

- having a sense of humour

- sharing

- having fun

- partnership

- being a role model

- caring

- being loved and loving

- seeing things through to the end

- patience

- giving time

- putting others first

- communication

- being there

1
Becoming a Dad

Becoming a father, that is simple. Being one is hard.

WHAT IS FATHERING?

A woman does not need to learn how to be a mother. She might be an inadequate mother for a variety of reasons, but she knows the essential meaning of the job. A man always has to learn how to be a father.

Our role model is our own father, but although most of us will use our father as a yardstick, we want to be closer to our children. The image of the authoritarian and disciplinarian father has been radically challenged in most societies, including our own. Until relatively recently, fathers had little to do with the upbringing of their children, but attitudes have changed dramatically. In 1940, fathers were generally not present at the birth of their children; by 1980, 92 per cent of all would-be fathers attended the birth.

The roles of men and women in a relationship are also changing. The traditional role of a man and father going out to work and earning the money to provide for his 'wife and children' while the 'wife' took care of the home and nurtured the children, has radically changed because of overall changes in society. Women had few rights and little equality with men seventy years ago: their role was clearly defined as mother and bearer of children. That has long gone, women are equal to men and have ambitions and expectations, and they have challenged the 'old role'. In many couples both partners work and both are important to the income of the family. Man has also developed and has wanted and welcomed this equality, wanted to be actively involved in the upbringing of his children, and share the responsibilities.

Men and women think differently and how they tackle parenting is different. As the child's first physical contact is with his/her mother, the mother more often than not sets the foundation for how the child is going to be raised. Men naturally take the lead from their partners and/or adopt the 'traditional' image of the father.

Yes, women do go through the nine-month period involved in physically producing a baby. It is interesting to note that 'to father' is generally understood as simply meaning to sire, to be the producer of sperm which fertilises the egg which becomes the child. It implies that to be a father only requires you to perform the sex act and leave. But 'to mother' is understood as meaning to comfort, nurture, love. However, apart from the physical production, parenting should be seen as involving equality, a shared joy, job, experience. This book explores the practicalities and needs of children and how as a father you can contribute to this experience.

CHOICE OR ACCIDENT?

It is assumed that you know how babies are made. If not, you should definitely go straight to a good sex education guide!

Becoming a father does not mean you are married or even in a stable relationship. It is preferable if you *are* in a secure relationship but this is not an essential requirement. Choosing to be a father usually means that you are in a steady partnership or married. You have discussed the question of having children, and have made a choice with the woman of your choice.

Or it was a sudden shock. One day you were happily going along, and then you were told the news, 'I'm going to have a baby, and it's yours!'

The full realisation of becoming a father does not hit until the baby is born, whether by choice or accident.

There are many men who run away at the news. This book is not a psychology textbook that debates the duties and responsibility of absent dads, but tackles the issues for fathers who want to be dads, although some of you have or had to get used to the idea.

For first time fathers, or second or third time around dads, the shock to the system can be quite alarming.

Case study: Martin becomes a dad

'My first reaction, when I was told, was how did it happen? I know that is stupid, but I was sure my wife was on the pill. It was so sudden. Then I started to feel proud. I could produce children, I had a sense of virility. I started to see all these men with children, and said to myself, I'm going to be a dad. I found the pregnancy period confusing and felt sometimes completely out of it, but when I saw our daughter, Lauren, being born, I was amazed and a real joy came over me. It is difficult to describe. It was real and part of me.'

THINKING ABOUT THE BABY

Soon you're going to have a baby! Well, your partner, wife, girlfriend, is going to have a baby. Maybe you have one already. You're excited, confused. You start listening to friends and relatives when they talk about bringing up a child. Everyone seems to want to give some advice. It may surprise you to hear that the more people have studied different methods of bringing up children the more they have come to the conclusion that what a good mother and father instinctively feel like doing for their babies is usually best.

Fathers and mothers don't really find out how to care for and manage children from books and lectures. We learn the basics from the way we were cared for as children. The rest we learn from practical experience. Don't be afraid of your baby. Enjoy the children as they are – that's how they'll grow up best. Babies are not frail ('I'm so afraid I'll hurt her if I don't handle her right!'). They are tougher than you think.

Men react to the news of pregnancy with various feelings:

Positive thoughts
- protectiveness towards the 'partner'
- increased pride in relationship
- increased pride about their virility (men do worry about this)
- anticipatory enjoyment of a child.

Negative thoughts
A feeling of being left out, expressed as:

- grumpiness towards partner
- wanting to spend more evenings with men friends
- flirting with other women.

Why has my wife changed so much since she became pregnant?
A pregnant woman goes through the equivalent of an operation. Pregnancy involves enormous hormonal changes. She will of course also be anxious about the baby.

UNDERSTANDING YOUR PARENTAL RESPONSIBILITY

A father is a parent and to that extent has a responsibility for his children. How we interpret this role is something we learn from our parents and examples around us. In fact, formal **parental**

responsibility is a new legal concept introduced by the **Childrens Act 1989**. It is defined as:

> All the rights, duties, powers, responsibilities and authority which by law a parent of a child has in relation to the child and his property.

Rights and responsibilities
Here are some of the rights and duties a parent has:

- to protect and maintain your child

- to see your child attends school between five and sixteen years old

- to choose the child's schooling

- to ensure your child receives medical treatment

- to name your child

- to consent to your child's marriage if he/she is aged under eighteen

- to represent your child

- to decide where your child is to live

- to choose your child's religion

- to discipline your child.

Who has legal parental responsibility of a child?
Mothers and married fathers automatically have legal responsibility for their children. In the event of divorce, the courts have to decide on the rights of each parent. Unmarried fathers do not have any legal rights over their children unless they go to court and get a parental responsibility order or acquire custody. However, both married and unmarried fathers have a duty to maintain their children.

Is being a parent a job?
Yes. It is not a job that you apply for in the normal way, and often it is not recognised as such. The fact is, however, that being a parent is very important and the skills you acquire are far ranging.

UNDERSTANDING THE JOB OF BEING A PARENT

The first step to understanding the job of parenting is to ask what are the accepted aims in the society we live in, in relationship to our children. If you look around the world, whatever the culture, whether it is Muslim, Jewish or our own, the general aims of being a parent are the same. Education may be defined differently. It may mean teaching children to read and write. It may also mean teaching children to tend sheep or fetch water.

Figure 1 is a list of the things that you and the mother of your child do every day as a parent. You may have different words but the path is the same whatever your background. You may have particular views of method, due to social and cultural upbringing, but the aim is simply to bring your children up to be healthy and happy individuals.

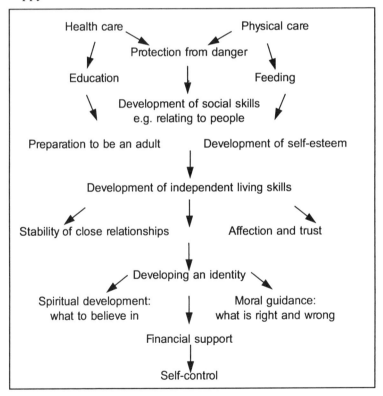

Fig. 1. The job of being a parent.

CHANGING YOUR LIFE

Children change your life! They really do, that's an understatement. Your life as a young adult circulates around you. When children come along, before you know it you are circulating around them. Look at the chart below, which lists some of the things that fathers find themselves doing. How many of these do *you* do – or do you *think* you may do (if you are not yet a father)?

Things fathers can do	I do it:		
	Sometimes	A lot	Never
Give bottles and solid foods			
Change nappies and clothes			
Wipe tears and noses			
Bath and put to bed			
Read stories			
Mend toys			
Patch up quarrels			
Help with questions about homework			
Explains rules and assign duties and see that they are carried out			
Shopping			
Cooking and serving			

LOOKING AT THE STATISTICS

The present-day dad is very different from his father. Statistics show a clear trend that men are taking a more active role in the care of their children. This has to be seen alongside the trend of women being more economically active.

- In 1981, 53 per cent of all women aged sixteen and over were economically active, 8 per cent higher than in 1971. In 1996, half the workforce in the UK were women.

- In eight out of ten married or cohabiting couples the washing and ironing is usually done by the women, whereas in around half the couples the shopping is either shared equally or done together.

Changing attitudes towards father being present at birth					
	1940s	1950s	1960s	1970s	1980s
Mothers wanted fathers to be present at birth	14.3%	38.9%	50%	73.1%	95%
Father was present	none	8.5%	32.%	64%	92%

- In 1950, the National Survey of Health and Development reported that one-third of mothers received some regular help from the father or 'someone else'. In 1975, this had risen to 50 per cent, e.g. fathers contributing to shopping and housework, taking children to school, etc.

How is the father's role changing?

A study of over 12,000 married fathers in 1980 showed a third had a partner/wife who worked. A third of these fathers took an active role in caring for the children whilst the mother worked.

However, 40 per cent of the fathers studied came home after work to a sleeping child. An American study of middle-class fathers of one-year-old children showed that they spent not more than 20 minutes a day with their children. So although roles are changing, women, even when working, still undertake the main carer role.

All these studies, however, seem to show two distinctive groups of fathers in stable relationships.

- fathers who cannot or do not play much of a personal role in bringing up their children or the day-to-day running of the household.

- fathers who play an active part in bringing up their children, by getting home before bedtime, running the home, caring for the children if mum goes out to work.

Statistics indicate the latter is becoming more common.

RELATING TO THE MOTHER OF YOUR CHILD

Years ago, the traditional image of the family was the man being the breadwinner, and the wife at home looking after the children and all the domestic responsibilities. This image is still around but is not one the majority of women want. They want, as most modern men do, a real partnership that enables both partners to achieve their ambitions and goals and together make a family within which to share responsibilities. Women have the full responsibility of carrying the child for nine months until it is born, and a would-be dad has to learn the art of supportive friend as well as lover.

When your baby is born and as your child grows, the role of parents is something both you and your partner will evolve and decide. You need to relate to and respect the mother of your children, whether your relationship stands the test of time or sadly ends. Whatever happens, your children will always be yours and you have created them together with their mother. How you relate to her will affect them for better or worse in the long term.

PARENTING AS CHILDREN GROW UP

Parenting is a life-long commitment. It doesn't stop after the age of five, as many of the baby magazines would have us believe. You will still be a father when you become a grandfather or even a greatgrandfather. Parents need to give their children a sense of security, enabling them to develop and grow. Security is not about whether you have a large house and money in the bank, but is a state of mind, providing self-esteem and confidence.

CONTINUING AS A FATHER AFTER RELATIONSHIPS END

The structure of families is rapidly changing with one out of four households now headed by a single parent. There is a large increase in second relationships and stepfamilies. It is hoped that you are able to maintain a long-term relationship with the mother of your children, but whatever happens, your role as a father has to continue.

CASE STUDIES: INTRODUCTION

Let us now introduce five dads whose experiences we will be following in the succeeding chapters. Each has become a father in different circumstances and each interprets his role differently, but all deeply care for and love their children.

Carlton and Dawn planned their family

Carlton became a father at seventeen whilst at school, but he lost contact with the mother until sixteen years later. Carlton now has regular contact with his daughter who is now eighteen.

Carlton met Dawn at college and both qualified as lawyers. They lived with each other for three years before deciding to have children, although Dawn had problems and had to have fertility treatment. They did not want to get married. Dawn had maternity leave when their first child was born and returned to work after six months. She went part-time when their second was born, two years later. Carlton and Dawn planned their family and share most of the chores around the children and home, although they do have a nanny when Dawn goes to work.

Stephen was a dad at seventeen

Stephen left school at fifteen, the year before they put the school-leaving age up to 16. He worked in a factory, where he met Kay. They went out with each other for about six months, when she became pregnant – she was sixteen. Kay's parents were very angry and kicked Kay out. Stephen's mum was supportive and Stephen and Kay started to live together at her home. Paul was born, and a year later they married. Everyone around them thought they would soon break up, but in fact their marriage has lasted nearly twenty years, bringing four more children. Stephen went to night school and is now a production foreman. He did leave Kay for a year after their second child, but came back.

Tony is divorced

Tony was married for eight years and with his ex-wife Claire, they have two boys, David and Martin. Tony and Claire divorced four years ago, after Tony had an affair with someone ten years younger. He moved out and lived with his proposed new partner for two years, but they have since broken up and he now lives alone. Claire was on her own for two years and now has remarried to Michael. Tony has the boys every other weekend, and sees them once a week when he takes them to a swimming club. He also has them for one week at Christmas and for three weeks in the summer.

Martin is a single parent dad

Martin is a forty-year-old lone father of three children, Lauren (fifteen), Steven (eleven) and Mark (ten). He has been on his own for eight years. Martin was married to Amanda for eight years, when suddenly she left through severe post-natal depression. She could not cope with looking after three small children and decided to go and live with her parents, initially to rest. She never returned and eventually they divorced. Martin worked full-time as a manager of a security company, but because of the unsocial hours, had to give it up and now relies on state benefit. He works part-time in a youth club and is training to become a full-time youth leader. Amanda visits the children regularly. Martin and Amanda have a strong friendship but have no intention of coming together again.

'It doesn't matter whether you are a man or a woman, you still face the same emotional problems and the loneliness. Whoever you are, the pleasure of being there for your kids is simply that of watching them grow up and seeing how they relate to you.'

Philip is a house husband

Philip married Jane ten years ago, and they have two daughters, Mary (eight) and Anne (six). Philip is a bricklayer by trade, and during the housing boom, had plenty of work. Jane stayed at home to care for the children. However, the building trade started to decline and Philip was laid off between jobs. Jane decided to return to work in order to supplement their income and as she had qualifications and experience in book-keeping she secured a reasonable job in a clothing factory. Soon Philip was at home full-time caring for the children and as Jane could earn more money than him, it was agreed that their roles should reverse.

'Fathers miss out on so much. They may come home at night after the children are in bed and at the weekend when they would normally see them they are tired and trying to recuperate from work. There's little point in having children when you are too tired to enjoy them and I believe that I now enjoy a relationship with my two that I would not have had if I had been the breadwinner.'

DISCUSSION POINTS

1. Write down a list of all the things that have to be done for your children and put your name or your partner's against who does what.

2. Think of when you were a child, and what you liked and disliked about your own father.

3. Talk to your male friends who have children and ask them about their views on fatherhood. Talk to your partner and children.

2
What Kind of Father am I?

This may seem an odd question to ask. A father is a father. Well, are you a caring father? Do you live in a two-parent household? Are you a divorced dad who only sees his children at weekends or a divorced dad that does not see his children at all? Being a father is an individual state; each father is different because of variations in background and status. You will define your role as a father according to how you saw your own father, as well as in the light of beliefs and culture. Your relationship with the mother of your child/children will determine much of your role. If you are married and live in a house with your wife and children, both of you will define the role of father, but if you are unmarried, the boundaries could be different since the legal responsibility of parenting remains with the unmarried mother. A divorced or 'absent' dad has to totally redefine his role. A single parent dad has to take on the day-to-day role of both parents like any lone parent.

EXPLORING THE DIFFERENT ROLE MODELS

The key to self-discovery of what kind of father you are is to look at yourself through the eyes of your children. This can be done in three ways:

- Think of your own childhood. What did you like and dislike about your dad?

- Ask your children, if they are old enough, what they like and dislike about you.

- Explore what you do and what your father did, by completing the short questionnaire below.

	You	Your dad	What your child wants/needs
Attended ante-natal courses			
Was at birth			
Get children up			
Feed children			
Cook for children			
Wash clothes			
Take children to school			
Read stories			
Take them out on day trips			

What kind of father am I?

The role of father will be determined by you and your partner and is a job which will last until you die. However, it will be influenced by the structure of your relationship with the mother of your children; your age – now, and when you became a father, and the size of your family.

A FAMILY WITH TWO PARENTS

Whatever the papers and television tell you, most children are brought up in households with two parents, the majority of whom are married. Whether you describe this situation as traditional or conventional, it is what most of us strive for: a family with two parents and children. It is what the majority of adults were brought up in. The family, like all aspects of society, is changing to meet our and society's needs. We challenge it every day in the simplest of ways, from arguing over who should do the shopping to negotiating evenings out.

Our children have far more information and role images than in the past and are now not passive partners in a family: they tell you what they want and expect. It can be a shock.

Economic status and finance may determine whether you as a father are the sole breadwinner or whether both you and your partner work. Women now also choose to work for their own interest rather than simply for financial reasons.

SEPARATED AND DIVORCED

Over 200,000 marriages break up each year and this figure is rising. One out of four families are headed by a lone parent. Traditionally women have automatically been given custody of their children, but court attitudes are slowly changing and more fathers are fighting for custody and bringing up their children as lone parents. **Shared parenting** is also becoming more popular.

However, the father only seeing his children periodically is the norm in such situations and over 50 per cent lose all contact with their children. This is a bad thing not only for the children but also for the father. 'Parental Loss' syndrome is now recognised as an illness.

Many dads who have no contact with their children from their first relationship, remarry and have new children or take over as stepdad and care for someone else's.

THE ROLE OF THE ABSENT FATHER

Even if you have left the 'family' household, or perhaps were never in it, you are still a father and this is very important to every child. Children who grow up without contact with their father have repeatedly stated, in a variety of studies, that this has caused them emotional problems in adult life. Many go on a mission to find their father.

Case study: Carlton meets his daughter

'I was seventeen when I had my first child. I was a bit of a lad and put it around a bit. My mum and dad didn't approve, but it seemed normal amongst my mates. I lost contact with "mum and child" after the birth and they were getting money from social security. Sixteen years later, I was in a secure relationship and had children with my girlfriend, Dawn, and up popped my daughter. There she was standing on the doorstep, saying 'Hello dad". I was gobsmacked. What do you say? I was full of mixed emotion. One of joy, she was such a good-looking girl, full of life. But also sheer fear. The fear of being blamed for deserting "mum and child" all those years ago and the fear of upsetting Dawn. She knew, but knowing is one thing and being faced with your boyfriend's daughter is another. Sally told me she had hated me, but felt she had to meet me, to put one of the pieces of the jigsaw puzzle into place.'

CHANGING ROLES

Our society is radically changing and this includes the economic structure we live in. Throughout the 1970s and 1980s, jobs in traditional 'male' dominated industries declined whereas many of the new jobs created were targeted at women. This has meant that in many areas of the UK, men are unemployed and women are working. The woman has become the financial breadwinner in the traditional sense. The husband has had to become the supportive partner and care for the children and the home. Many couples are also making the clear decision of role reversal, as they are recognising that equality is about recognition of skills. Many women have better prospects in the workplace and are happier in that environment, whereas many men are preferring to be at home with the kids. Work patterns are also changing to enable people to work from home which means that both 'financial' and 'domestic' work can be combined, with possibly both parents being at home.

Case study: Philip is at home
Philip had to care for the children when it became obvious that his wife had a better chance to hold down a job. He now cares full-time for his daughters, while his wife works at a local factory as a wages clerk.

'The ideal for us would have been job sharing but that was impossible. When we made our decision, companies just didn't entertain the idea of paternity leave and our jobs and skills are different anyway. We had to make the choice of role reversal for financial reasons but now looking back I am glad I had the opportunity. I would never have got to know my kids working in the building trade. Other countries such as Scandinavia, which allows fathers to take time off work to be with their children, seem to be miles ahead of us in this respect and many more men appear to be choosing to spend more time at home.'

FATHERHOOD OUTSIDE MARRIAGE

In 1994 32 percent of live births were outside marriage, which means a third of new fathers in the UK are not married to the mother of their children.

All mothers and married fathers have automatic legal rights to their children and have legal responsibility for them. Unmarried fathers do not have an automatic right although under the **Child Support Act**, they have a duty to maintain the child.

As the unmarried father of my child, do I have any rights?
If you are not married to the child's mother you don't have an automatic right to custody or access, and if the child's mother doesn't want you to have access it will be necessary for you to obtain a court order. You still have to pay maintenance.

BECOMING A WIDOWER

'There was absolutely no advance warning and when she died, it felt as if half of me had died with her, but the other half had to tell the children.'

In 1994 in the UK, there were 30,000 widowed lone fathers and 60,000 widowed lone mothers.

The father quoted above had to face the problems of single parenthood, while at the same time grieving for the death of his partner. Sometimes the death has happened suddenly and there is no time to prepare for widowed parenthood. It is just thrown at you. Other times, death has been through a traumatic long illness.

SINGLE PARENT FATHERS

Can a man really bring up his children alone?
Men are very able to bring up their children alone, and 10 per cent of all single parent families are headed by a man.

Men tend to become lone parents when there is no other choice available to the children, i.e. their mother dies, leaves home or becomes severely incapacitated through illness or disability. However, more men are actively contesting the custody of their children and the courts are not automatically awarding custody to the mother as in the past. With the move to conciliation and taking the fault aspects out of divorce, there is a likelihood that more children will come under the immediate welfare of their father. There is a strong development in the concept of shared parenting where the child spends half the time with the father and half with the mother.

Case study: Martin brings up his children alone
Martin is bringing up his three children alone, after this wife left

because of post-natal depression. He never imagined he was going to be a single parent.

'The whole system works on the basis that children should be with their mother. My thoughts were immediately that for men to be at home caring for the children was not natural. Men should be out in the world of work, creating role models for their children of what it is to be male. Men as well as women *can* take care of children. Lone fathers are pioneers, opening up the boundaries around the question of who can do childcare. I firmly believe men and women's roles are interchangeable and men are as capable as women of nurturing children. Lone fathers resemble mothers more than they differ from them. We may have different styles of parenting to women but they are no better or no worse.'

BECOMING A STEPDAD

This is becoming a normal occurrence, as more people divorce and find new partners. There are 1.4 million single parents in the UK, and a proportion of these find new partners every year and emerge as a stepfamily. A stepdad simply means that you marry or live with someone who has children from a previous relationship.

Unless your new partner is a widow, there will be a 'birth' father somewhere in the background, and the way the relationship ended and any conflict was (or was not) resolved will partly determine your relationship with your new partner's children. They will initially see you either as a threat or as a bonus. It could be that you already have children but you are now divorced and they live with their mum. As your new partner has children, you have to combine the role of 'absent' father with stepdad, and 'birth' dad (yet again) if you have more children with your new partner.

Sounds complicated but this situation is becoming more normal. Michael Rosen, in his excellent book *Goodies and Daddies*, describes his multiple role as absent, step, and second time around father with 'Your children are fighting my children and our child started it.'

Case study: Michael becomes stepdad of Tony's sons
Tony and Claire divorced four years ago and after two years Claire married Michael, whom she met through work. Michael is four years older than Claire and it is his first marriage. He has no children from any previous relationships. Claire cannot have any more children.

'I love Claire very much, and obviously I love her sons. She was very worried when I first met them, as she felt they were bound to hate me. In fact we made friends quickly. Their father has regular contact and Claire makes sure I don't get involved in the children's arrangements. When we married and started living together I was very apprehensive as I was not sure what I should do. Should I discipline the boys when they did something wrong? What should they call me? I was very surprised one day, when the youngest called me dad. They call me Michael in the main. I get on with their dad probably better than Claire, and that helps a great deal.'

BEING A GAY FATHER

Society is opening up, too fast or too slow, depending on your own personal view, and one of the taboos that is being broken, is being gay and being a parent. Being a good parent is nothing to do with your sexuality. However, we do live in a society that regards the norm as children being cared for by a married couple (man and woman). So you as a gay father are breaking two taboos at once.

Will my sexuality affect the development of my children?
Research into gay parenting shows few differences between children brought up by gay and lesbian parents and their heterosexually reared schoolmates. It is important for children to know their parents are happy and relatively stress-free which is hard to achieve if you are under stress from a marriage break-up or because you are coming to terms with your sexuality.

While it is preferable that parents place a high priority on their children's needs, this does not exclude considering your own needs for personal fulfilment in whatever sort of adult relationship you desire. Common sense suggests that people who are contented in themselves are more likely to be able to be generous and supportive parents.

DISCUSSION POINTS

1. Explore what kind of father you are compared with your own father. Use the checklist on page 24.

2. Talk to your children and ask them what they like doing with you, and what they expect their father to do.

3. Discuss with the mother of your future child what kind of father she would like you to be.

3
Experiencing the Birth

Fatherhood starts at conception, whether planned or not, and is confirmed at the birth. It is nine months from conception to birth, but by the time you know it will be eight to seven months away from the miracle of seeing your child appear on the horizon, or, the normal way for nearly 90 per cent of all fathers these days, emerge from your partner's womb. The waiting period of pregnancy is relatively short but can seem ages and very unreal, especially if it is your first child. You have played an important part in the creation of your child but it's your partner who takes the full physical responsibility of pregnancy and birth. It can be a very confusing time and it is often pretty hard to fathom what your role is. Are you simply the breadwinner, paying for the large amount of extras that now take up the shopping list? Or do you have to emerge as a very supportive carer to the mother of your future child? Only you and your partner can answer these questions and determine your level of involvement.

RECEIVING THE GOOD NEWS

You may have discussed having children with your partner, but until she tells you that she may be pregnant and this is confirmed by the doctor, the reality of being a father may have not fully occurred to you.

Case study: Tony learnt the good news
'We had been married for about a year when my wife told me one day that she thought she was pregnant. A week later it was confirmed. My initial reaction was panic. We were married and had talked many times about children, but I suppose it never properly entered my head that we would really have any. We had planned our life around ourselves, we both had jobs and a good social life, and then this bombshell came. It was a mixture of ego (I wasn't shooting blanks), happiness that we were going to have a child, and blind panic on all issues like, could we afford to care for a child, was our

30

flat big enough, would I still be able to go out and play snooker?

'Sounds selfish, but my head was full of these things, although I just reassured my wife that I was overjoyed. Soon everyone seemed to know and the more people congratulated us the more I felt confident this was a wonderful thing that was happening to me.'

UNDERSTANDING THE STAGES OF PREGNANCY

It is hard for many men to take in the full impact of a child being born, especially if it is the first. Once a baby is conceived there is a period of nine months when the baby develops inside the mother. This is observed by you, the father, through the visible change of size, shape and weight of the expectant mother. A woman gains about 13 kg in a normal pregnancy. Her hormones and emotions change, and both of you will start to see your way of life change radically.

The chart below shows the stages of growth and development of an embryo to a foetus to a baby.

Month	The Baby	The Mother
1	Human embryo is formed.	Possible morning sickness.
2	Embryo is growing to human likeness, now called foetus. The main structures of the body are more or less in place and the heart is beating.	
3	Nerves and muscles are developing rapidly. Foetus weights about 55 g (2oz).	
5	The mother is able to feel the baby's movement. The heartbeat can be heard. Foetus weighs about 350 g ($^3/_4$ lb).	Getting larger and more tired.
7	Development is almost complete. During the next two months the length will double and the weight increase three times.	

What is morning sickness?

Hormone changes are responsible for the feelings of sickness felt by some women in the early months of pregnancy, usually in the morning, sometimes in the evening, or at other times. Feelings of sickness (nausea) are much more common than actually being sick (vomiting).

What is a premature baby?

A premature baby is one which is born before it is expected, perhaps as early as the seventh month. Premature babies are very small and weak and need special care.

PREPARING FOR THE BABY

Children are not cheap and a new baby requires a great deal to enable him/her to grow and develop fully. Look at the list below of a few of the things you and your partner will have to buy or acquire. It is only a guide but will give you an idea of what is involved. You will also need to prepare a room or space for the baby.

Shopping list for baby

Cot	Blankets
Baby bath and mat	Waterproof sheeting
Towels	Sheets
Safety pins	Scales
Thermometer	Pram or buggy
Cotton wool	Dummies
Vitamin drops	Playpen
Baby soap	Baby powder
Disposable nappies	Baby lotion
Car seat	Baby oils
Baby carrier	Sore bottom cream
Night gowns	Bottles, teats
Vests	Bottle warmer
Babygro suits	Sterilising unit
Jumpers	Long-handled spoon
Outdoor clothes	Set of measuring spoons
Bibs	Bottle brush
Caps, bonnets, mittens	Highchair

SURVIVING ANTE-NATAL CLASSES

Most childbirth classes now have one 'fathers' evening, but the best pre-birth classes include fathers in most if not all the classes – for those who want to go.

The reality of the pregnancy period is that it can be very difficult at times, and the thought of going to ante-natal classes with your partner can be absolutely terrifying. But it will be OK, more and more men are going and you will be surprised by the variety of men. The image of new age hippy man going through the whole pregnancy experience has long gone and in fact was never a reality. The reality is that the 'male' world that we create and is created for us tends to label certain things as 'sissy'. As boys we played with cars not dolls, or if we did play with dolls it was probably in secret. This 'secret' of a caring and sensitive side makes us feel vulnerable at times and the thought of exposing this part of ourselves in a public arena can be frightening.

At the end of the day, however, the most important thing is what you and your partner want to do. Going to ante-natal classes can be an effective way of learning what is happening to your partner and how you can help. It is also a good way of meeting people in the same boat and sharing your experiences. You will be surprised how many men feel the same.

What happens at the ante-natal clinic?
Your partner will go regularly to have her weight checked, blood tests, blood pressure taken, urine tests, and examinations. All of this is to make sure she and the baby are in a healthy condition. At later stages the doctor listens to the baby's heartbeat, while ultrasound scans produce visible pictures of the baby in the mother's womb.

UNDERSTANDING YOUR PARTNER'S FEELINGS

For most men, their partner's pregnancy is a confusing period, especially the first time. You have less than eight months to prepare for this arrival, as you watch the future mother visibly growing. She will also start to experience a great hormonal change which expresses itself in a variety of ways.

What are hormones?
Hormones are the secretions of the endocrine glands, and to a great extent they govern what we are, our size, shape and temperament.

Hormone activity can make us happy or sad, energetic or slow moving. From conception and during pregnancy hormones play a very special role both physically and emotionally. Much depends on their correct balance and function, and their activity is beyond our conscious control. This last fact needs to be stressed, for your wife may often feel guilty because she cannot control the fluctuations of mood that she finds herself experiencing during pregnancy. One day she is bright, happy and excited, full of joy and anticipation at the prospect of having a baby. The next she may be depressed and crying, wishing she had never got pregnant at all.

My wife's moods change all the time, what can I do?

You need to have a sense of humour during pregnancy. Your wife will go through a range of moods, and her behaviour will change, ranging from laughter to uncontrollable tears. She may snap at you. It is all part of the hormonal change and part and parcel of pregnancy. Normally the most emotional and fragile time for your partner will be the first and last three months of pregnancy.

What is ante-natal depression?

Most people have heard of post-natal depression, but many women get extremely depressed during pregnancy. It can be that the would-be mum doesn't know whether she wants the child, is irritated by friends and relatives getting excited. Give comfort, and boost her confidence.

Will sex have to stop during pregnancy?

Let's be honest, this is what many men fear. Many leave their partners at this stage, as the thought of nine months without sex is too much. Being pregnant, however, does not mean a woman cannot have sex. In fact you can have sex right up to the birth. You have to be a bit imaginative about position.

Women do not necessarily feel like having sex during their pregnancy, but this should not be seen as rejection of their partner. Look at it this way, would you feel sexy with a baby in your stomach? The amazing thing is that if you are supportive and understanding, you might find your partner feeling less guilty, and suddenly full of sexual desire.

CARING FOR YOUR PARTNER THROUGH PREGNANCY

Your partner is going to need a lot of care and support through pregnancy. This is not going to be easy. As the woman has to take all the literal weight of the physical aspect of birth, the man's role gets a bit blurred.

The most important role of future fathers is to be as understanding as possible:

- Try to get to know what is going on.

- Talk to your partner.

- Go with her to ante-natal classes.

- Give comfort to your partner (no not sex!). Give her support and boost her confidence.

- Once she knows that you understand her feelings, she'll start talking to you. And the more you both talk about your feelings, fears and anxieties the better it will be for both of you.

- Pregnancy is a waiting game, and like waiting in a very long supermarket queue, not easy.

- See life as a combination of good and bad, happy and unhappy, easy and difficult.

- Learn to share, understand and adapt.

ATTENDING THE BIRTH

It is now very acceptable for fathers to be present at the birth of their babies, though this might not be the initial choice of some men. You need to be a participant not merely an observer.

The birth of a child takes places in three main stages:

Stage One – The neck of the uterus opens. The waters break. Regular and strong contractions occur.

Stage Two – The baby passes through the birth canal.

Stage Three – The baby becomes a separate person. The umbilical cord is cut.

Case study: Martin is at the birth

'I was close to my wife and I wanted to be there and she wanted me. It was a bit fraught at first and there was a lot of hanging around waiting for it to happen. I sat by the bed and watched this machine which was wired up to Amanda's tummy and you heard this beep beep of the baby. Suddenly, it stopped, I thought the baby had died. The nurse told me casually that it did just go off, and the baby was OK, and all dads made the same mistake. It seemed to be an in joke – how to catch first time dads out. I was mortified. My wife was more relaxed than me. When her contractions started, I held her hand, and her waters broke, and she was wheeled into the delivery room.

'There seemed to be lots of people buzzing about and with one almighty push which looked as if Amanda was going to explode, Lauren was born. I saw the long cord and said out loud "It's a boy!" "No, she isn't, it's a girl, that's the umbilical cord" was the reply. Another regular duff dad observation to add to the nurses' score. I was over the moon, then all of a sudden, the baby was being wheeled off in one direction and my wife in another and I'm being told to come back in the morning. It was the middle of the night, it was cold and there were no buses to get home. I found a phone box to ring my dad. "I'm a dad, dad". "Do you know what the time is?" was the reply. I felt alone. I sat down on a park bench and tried to tell a tramp, but he wanted to go to sleep. I got back to the hospital at 8 am. I was so happy to see Amanda and Lauren.

'It was exciting and very emotional, especially the wonderful moment when the baby emerged after all the effort and patience. Part of the time I felt useful and part of the time in the way – about fifty-fifty. But I wouldn't have missed it for anything.'

Can we decide how our child is born?
Hospitals differ a great deal on policy and facilities. Ask your midwife and doctor before the birth and discuss what you want. It is possible still to have your child at home, but you may have problems finding a doctor who will agree to this. Don't get bamboozled by the professionals. Decide with your partner what you both want, and you will find a way. Being involved will make you much closer to your children.

What is natural childbirth?
More and more women are wanting their babies by natural childbirth. This means they want the least possible anaesthesia so that they can participate actively in the delivery and see the baby being born.

What is a caesarean section?
This is an operation to remove the baby from the uterus. It is carried

out when the birth canal is too narrow, or the baby is very late, or the health of the baby or mother makes immediate delivery necessary.

What help do we get in the first few weeks?
The midwife will visit every day for ten days after the birth. A health visitor will call and see the new mum and baby after this period. She will advise the mother on how to keep herself and her baby healthy, check that the baby is making normal progress, and advise on feeding.

What if it is twins?
Doctors will usually know whether you are going to have one or more children early on in the pregnancy and you will have time to adjust to the idea. Special care and attention is given to multiple births. However, it is a good idea to make contact with the **Twins and Multiple Birth Association** (see the Useful Addresses section).

My wife is in her late thirties. Will she have problems?
More and more women are deciding to have children in their thirties and forties. Medical practices are now very advanced and women can have babies much later perfectly healthily. However, doctors will take special care and there will be certain tests, in particular to discover whether the future baby has Down's Syndrome, a form of learning difficulty. Women aged over 35 are more prone to give birth to Down's Syndrome babies. You would be fully consulted about any tests and their implications a long time before the birth. More rest is needed for older 'first time mums' and they are likely to have a longer stay in hospital.

How do I register the birth?
A baby has to be registered by the parents within six weeks (or three weeks in Scotland). The name under which the child is to be brought up must be given to the Registrar of Births. A birth certificate will then be issued. If the parents are married to each other, either of them can register the child. If the parents are not married to each other, then the child must be registered by the mother. If both the mother and father wish the father's name to be shown on the birth certificate, it's necessary for them both to be present when the child is registered.

KNOWING HOW TO SUPPORT YOUR PARTNER AFTER THE BIRTH

The answer to this question can only be given by your partner, and you need to ask her and listen. Your partner will come home with your new son/daughter after a few days, and you need to have prepared a warm house and welcome for them.

You will pick them up at the hospital and take them home by taxi or car. Birth is an exhausting business, and the sudden transformation from physically carrying a child for nine months to having to care for it night and day when it is born, although natural for a woman, is very traumatic.

Doing as much as you can on the domestic front in the first few weeks will be a great help.

CHANGING NAPPIES AND ALL OTHER PRACTICALITIES

It is much better to play with a baby than change the rear end, but everything is much simpler these days with the invention of the disposable nappy.

Regular day-to-day baby duties include:

- feeding and winding
- changing nappies and clothing
- bathing
- playing with them
- taking them for walks to get fresh air
- comforting and cuddling.

COMING TO TERMS WITH POST-NATAL DEPRESSION

After the birth many women suffer deep depression which can be caused by:

- hormonal changes
- bodily changes
- lifestyle changes
- tiredness
- household pressures.

This depression can be very severe and needs to be understood. What else can you do?

- Help with the baby.

- Support your partner emotionally.

- Seek medical advice and support.

There is a range of good support services for women and their families suffering from post-natal depression. The **Association of Post-Natal Illness** provides telephone support on a one-to-one basis for women suffering with post-natal depression from women who have recovered from it. The midwife and health visitor will also help.

UNDERSTANDING YOUR FEELINGS

This chapter tells you a lot about understanding your partner's feelings. However, your feelings are just as important and you shouldn't feel bad about the times when you feel deep resentment towards the baby and your partner. Having a baby and having children is a deeply emotional experience and it is often difficult for men to understand these feelings and express them. Our own fathers did not usually show signs of emotion and perhaps we think we shouldn't. This is wrong, you need to express your feelings and talk them over with your partner.

SORTING OUT YOUR LIFE AROUND YOUR NEW CHILD

The birth of a first baby is a stressful time in the relationship between a man and a woman and is often given as a reason for the breakdown of a marriage. Your life will change but you can and should be in control. Think about the following questions relating to *your* life and any changes that may be needed:

- Can you get paternity leave from work?

- Are there family and friends who can give practical support?

- Can you be flexible in your work hours so that you can be at home more?

- After maternity leave, what is going to happen when your wife goes back to work?

GETTING SUPPORT AND ADVICE

Getting good support and advice at the first stages of parenthood is essential. Thinking that you can go it alone will cause stress. There are a range of agencies and help groups prior to birth and some also provide after-care support and advice. The following are all readily available to help you:

- the mother of your child
- family and friends
- doctor
- midwife
- health visitor
- National Childbirth Trust.

DISCUSSION POINTS

1. Talk with your partner about the birth and the future baby.

2. Visit the ante-natal clinic with your partner and find out if there are sessions/classes for fathers.

3. Prepare a list of all the equipment and clothes you need for the future baby, and plan a room with your partner.

4
Caring for Children
Through the Years

Fatherhood is a life-long commitment and the birth is merely the start of a marathon of care and love. Each year of a child's growth brings new developments and problems.

There are key moments in a child's life which contribute to the child's learning process. These range from the birth to their first steps, from early speech to potty training, learning to read and write to starting playgroup and school. A parent is a navigator of a child and has to combine many roles into one, from principal carer to material provider, from teacher to taxi driver.

Without realising it, parents and children create a lifetime partnership which brings to both parties a sense of belonging, purpose and happiness. As a father you create, with the mother, the environment that enables your child to grow into a healthy adult, someone whom you respect and who respects you, whom you love and who loves you, and a mutual friend for life.

Your child will be influenced by you and his/her mother but also by friends, relatives, school and even TV (see Figure 2).

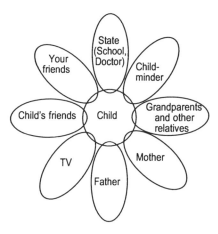

Fig. 2. The main influences on your child.

41

FINDING OUT WHAT A PARENT DOES

The essential role of a parent is providing a warm, happy and secure home. Your child is your responsibility, they are part of you and you have the care of them in partnership with their mother. It is important to understand the child's needs (see box below).

A child's needs			
Food	Home	Warmth	Clothing
	Love	Companionship	Protection
Support	Care	Training	Security

There are no fixed rules about what a parent does or doesn't do. You will have developed a view from your own childhood, and with your partner a broad unwritten plan of how you wish to care for your children will emerge. Traditionally a father's key role was being the financial provider, male role model and occasional source of discipline. Modern fathers, however, are moving towards being equal partners in the day-to-day care of their children. They also share the economic role as more and more women go out to work. Some fathers have adopted a total role reversal and care for the children at home while their partners go out to work.

Case study: Philip becomes a full-time parent

Philip job-swapped with his wife Jane, so that she can go out to work while he stays at home and looks after their two young daughters.

When the building trade started to decline, Jane got a job as a clerk in a clothing factory. 'We decided that as she was okay for work and I wasn't, I'd be the one to stay at home with the kids. It wasn't an easy decision, but circumstances forced it on me. For me, it was a big step to take over the mother's role.'

Mary, eight, and Anne, just turned six, now go to school. But when Philip took over their care, Mary was four and had started nursery school and Anne was only two-and-a-half and still in nappies.

At first, Philip was dumbfounded at the time it took to look after two young children as well as shopping and cleaning the house. 'I had no idea there was so much involved. Jane had to put up four pages of instructions on the fridge just so I could work out the washing and use the washing machine.'

Changing nappies proved the most challenging task. 'It was really hard getting used to that. The biggest thrill for me was getting Annie potty trained. I was really proud. I don't think I would have understood what a great moment that was if I hadn't been so closely involved. I actually had to train myself to take the baby with me every time I left the house. My pet hate has always been waiting outside the school gates for Mary and now Annie, too. None of the women have gone out of their way to make me feel just like one of the mums – but maybe that's my fault. I've got a bit of wall where I wait and I suppose I'm just part of the scenery now. But it feels a bit lonely.

'As for the children, since they've grown up with the slightly unusual arrangement of having dad at home and mum at work, they think nothing of it.

'You have to like children to do it, otherwise it wouldn't work. You can't lash out if they get on your nerves, you have to keep calm. It's not until you take over the reins yourself that you realise how much work there is. You really need a thirty-hour day. Most men have no idea what's involved.'

Remembering the key points
- Children are more important than housework.

- Parents are not meant to be perfect.

- No child is perfect.

- Do not expect too much of your children.

Knowing the routine
Study the child/parent daily routine chart on page 44 and complete it for yourself. Find out what goes on in your home and what is involved in caring for your children.

I've never had to do any housework. What does it involve?
You would be surprised how many men still have no knowledge of anything domestic. Their own mums did everything, and their expectation is their wife/girlfriend will do the same. Looking after a home and caring for a child involves a range of key tasks such as making meals, shopping for food, household goods and clothes, looking after a child's health, cleaning, laundry, ironing. The list is endless.

Children of all ages need a lot of care. The parent who is responsible for the everyday 'welfare and maintenance' of the

Weekdays

Time	Child	Parent
6.00–7.30 am	Wake up, play, watch TV.	Wake up, get up and dressed. Get children up.
7.30–8.00 am	Get up, wash or be washed, dress or be dressed, have breakfast.	Get breakfast, organise day, make packed lunches.
8.00–8.45 am	Get ready for school, go to school, be taken to school.	See children off to/or take them to childminder, play-group.

[Amend the above as necessary and complete the rest of the chart for your family:]

9.00–12 pm

12.00–1.30 pm

1.30–3.00 pm

3.00–3.30 pm

4.00–5.00 pm

5.00–6.00 pm

6.00–7.00 pm

7.00–8.00 pm

8.00–9.00 pm

9.00–10.00 pm

children has a range of often underrated tasks which call for a great deal of planning, decision-making and energy. Just think about what is involved in feeding and clothing your child on a daily basis.

CARING FOR BABY

The baby years are hectic and time-consuming, but a routine emerges of feeding, cleaning, bathing, playing and exercise. A mother does usually take the lead at this time, but you need to play your part. It is your baby too, and you should be involved. Love, cuddle, talk and play with your baby. Be involved in the feeding and cleaning. If you share in the roles, the baby (your child) will learn that both parents are important and it won't become totally reliant on one. This will not only strengthen your bond with your child but ease the strain put on your relationship by the new arrival. It is important to form your view of parenthood at the early stages, as this will establish the long-term pattern. Remember: children need a happy home, not a perfect one.

Case study: Tony changes nappies
'When the baby came home, I was over the moon, but very confused and soon quite resentful. Claire was giving David constant attention and was worried whether he would survive each night. She wanted to breastfeed, but had problems and was advised to use a bottle. I helped make up the feeds and shared the feeding. I was amazed how hungry David would get.

'The nappy changing took some getting used to. There weren't disposables at that time and we had to use towelling ones which were difficult to get clean and dry in the winter. The smell was awful, but you got used to it. I had never held a baby and learning to react to something which seemed fragile and that would cry in a moment was difficult. It is hard to describe, but there was this warm feeling of belonging that came over me when I held David.'

Why does our baby cry all the time?
Although it is not always possible to tell why a baby is crying, parents soon learn that it is probably for one of the following reasons: hunger, thirst, loneliness, discomfort, pain, tiredness, colic, dislike of dark, noise or boredom. It is usually hit or miss at first, finding out what a baby wants, as crying is his/her way of getting attention. If your baby persistently cries, seek advice from your doctor or health visitor.

BABIES BECOMING TODDLERS

Children grow very quickly, and before you know it they are running around, chattering away. The old cliché that 'it does not get easier', is very true. In fact, although babies need a lot of attention, they do go to sleep during the day, and often there are people around who long to hold them with an 'Oh, what a lovely baby!' But when they are running around all day, can climb out of the cot or playpen, that's when the fun starts. No longer can you just nip into a shop without a little hand grabbing something, or having a screaming fit. This transformation can be subtle but very traumatic.

Normal behaviour amongst two-year-olds

- 44 per cent attack their younger or older brother or sister

- 50 per cent eat too little

- 70 per cent resist going to bed

- 83 per cent whinge or nag

- 94 per cent constantly seek attention

- 95 per cent are stubborn

- 100 per cent are active and rarely stay still.

WHAT DO I DO AND WHAT DOES THE MOTHER DO?

The big question! Every family unit is unique and you should never try and imitate others, but develop your own parenting style with your partner. A dad cannot give birth or breastfeed, but you can do everything else. You might have a different level of skills, but don't confuse a lack of interest with a lack of skill.

I don't want to cook, as my mum always did it, so I cannot cook. You could learn. But does your partner want you to cook?

Can you do the following?

Cook	Boil a kettle	Iron clothes	Operate a washing machine
Drive a car		Read aloud	Make up a bottle feed
Feed a baby with a bottle		Change a nappy	Clean shoes
Shop	Carry a child	Administer first aid	Bath a child
Potty train	Make a doctor's appointment		Provide cuddles/love
	Keep children in order/discipline		

Make a list of what you do and your partner does:

Activity	Mother	Father	Someone else
Feed baby			
Cloth baby			
Change nappies			
Go to child clinic			

Could these jobs be shared more easily? Discuss them with your partner and children. Add to the list.

Fathers as role models
It is important to realise that how you are as a father provides an important role model to your children both male and female. Your presence throughout their childhood is very important as you are the first and principal male in their lives. Your actions and possible departure can have serious and adverse effects on them.

Father and daughter
A girl builds up a romantic attachment to her father, and it is on this basis that her relationship to the entire male sex is first orientated.

Father and son
A son's identification with his father is an important mechanism by which his character is developed. A small boy sees his father as the strongest, wisest, richest man in the world. He attempts to imitate his father's mannerisms, his tone of voice, his phrases. He plays imaginary games based on what he sees his father doing. He is learning to be a man, a husband, a father.

CHOOSING THE RIGHT CHILDCARE

This decision is usually made by the mother, but it is important for you to understand and have an involvement. Children need to mix with other children, and in the early years before school, outside childcare and nursery education is extremely important for the development of social skills. Chapter 11 provides full details of the kinds of childcare that are available.

CARING FOR, TEACHING AND LOVING YOUR CHILD

Parenting is far more than stuffing food down them, it is about nurturing, caring, teaching and loving. Most of us have some form of role model (good or bad) that influences how we want to bring up our children. Because of work, lack of money or sheer tiredness, you can often only carry out the basic parenting functions, but that special five minute hug, or cuddling up together for a TV film way past their bedtime, is very important and provides a great sense of security and belongingness for a child.

The pre-school years

The period between birth and the age of five is one of remarkable growth. The helpless baby turns into the lively, running, chattering, demanding five-year-old who is already mentally half-way to adulthood. Young children learn incredibly quickly in their first five years.

Children who have had some form of pre-school experience in nursery class or playgroup do have a distinct advantage when starting primary school, as they will have acquired a variety of social skills that are needed for school life.

School years

It is often a great relief when a child reaches school age and their life is directed between 9 am and 3.30 pm. These school years will develop them for their future lives.

Schooling is usually split into three stages, infant, junior and secondary. The UK education system tests children's ability through the National Curriculum at the ages of 7, 11 and 14. At 15–16 they take GCSE examinations which will determine what they will do in life.

At 16 children become young adults and can legally leave school, and have sex. However, parental responsibility continues under law until they reach their 18th birthday.

The school years can be more stressful than the first five years, as you have strong individuals emerging who take up more space and strongly invade yours. They argue and answer you back. They disobey orders. You are constantly challenged and asked to help with maths homework, that you don't understand. See this period as one of creative opportunity.

- Provide praise and opportunities that develop self-confidence.

- Provide discipline which is firm but fair.

- Provide opportunities to become independent and useful to others.

- Provide opportunities to be successful in some way and to take responsibility.

Surviving adolescence (ages 11–16)

Adolescents change from being dependent children to independent adults and then back again on an hourly basis. They will have an amazing discussion with you about the world, and five minutes later break down in a flood of tears as their favourite doll has been broken by their baby brother. This reflects the confusion of teenagers, as they use their families as the testing ground for their adulthood. It is emotionally very draining.

This period will bring up a range of issues relating to sexuality as they reach puberty, have their first sexual experiences, become attracted to the opposite sex or even their own sex, experiment with soft and hard drugs, rebel against you and society in general, and much much more. Remember that you were a teenager once and think of all the things you got up to.

I have a teenage daughter and she is having her first period, what do I do?
This is quite a common situation and usually an excuse for a quick exit. It highlights the lack of knowledge most men have about female concerns and the pure embarrassment and uncomfortableness that can arise. This shouldn't happen and issues such as your daughter's first period should be faced. Tampax, the leading producer of sanitary towels, publishes a useful booklet for dads. This is worth getting hold of – you could write to the company, ask your doctor or local Family Planning Clinic.

My son goes to youth club and they allow him to smoke
This is a good opportunity to make the point that teenagers will experiment and rebel, and will find places away from home to do it. They are becoming independent free-thinkers. Many youth clubs take the view that it is better to allow teenagers to come in rather than stay outside smoking. It is then possible for the leaders to talk to them openly about the bad effects of smoking, so that hopefully they will give up off their own free will. All parents have to go through this change, a development from instruction to negotiation.

CARING FOR CHILDREN WITH SPECIAL NEEDS

The term 'special needs' is very wide and can encompass Down's Syndrome to dyslexia, asthma to ataxia. One in five children have special needs.

Bringing up children is hard enough but giving further time and support to a child with special needs is extremely hard. In many cases it means that 100 per cent of one of the parent's time has to be concentrated caring for the child. If this is your situation, you deserve a lot of praise as well as a lot of support.

You've really got a lot to cope with. Don't be afraid or too proud to ask for help. There are people who can do a great deal for you, but you've got to let them know you are there. There are a range of organisations which can help you and these are listed at the back of this book.

FINDING THE RIGHT SUPPORT

As a father and parent you need and have a right to support and practical help, and it is available from a variety of sources.

The mother of your child, as well as family and friends are your natural advisers and supporters, but sometimes you need independent/unemotional advice.

It is always a good idea to seek out sources for support and advice when in fact you don't need it, then when you do you'll know exactly where to go. The two best local sources of information on what advice and support networks are in your area, are the **library** and the **Citizens Advice Bureau**. Both will have details of local support groups and of specialist advice on most subjects.

Parentline and **Parent Support Network** are increasingly improving services and recognising the needs of fathers. If you find yourself alone with your children, **Gingerbread** and the **National Council for One Parent Families** are a good starting point. There are also a number of **Father Support** Groups they can put you in touch with.

It could be that you become an 'absent' dad through relationship break-up, and you will find **Families Need Fathers** a good source of information, support and help.

The **National Stepfamilies Association** provides help for stepdads and has a number of useful publications.

Contact addresses and numbers can be found in the Useful Addresses section at the back of the book.

DISCUSSION POINTS

1. Study the child routine chart and develop your own with your partner.

2. Make a list of what your partner and you do in relation to the household and caring for the children. Could you do more?

3. Find out if there are local support groups in your area. Contact the Parent Support Network.

5
Relationship Break-up and the Children

More than 150,000 children see their families break up each year. Nearly 50 per cent of estranged parents, mainly fathers, will lose all contact with their children within two years of separation or divorce.

This book is not concerned with the rights and wrongs of parents splitting up, but it is concerned that children have a right to a continuing loving relationship with both their parents, and each parent has a unique contribution to make to their children's development, not only financially.

Children are deeply affected by the parents' split-up, possibly for the rest of their lives. As a father, and the person most likely to leave the family home, you need to be aware of the possible consequences of your actions, both in the short term and in the long term, and the effect on the children, however bitter you or your ex-partner may feel.

In an ideal world, all children would enjoy the loving presence of both parents. The reality is that many children living in one-parent families have little or no contact with their father.

The ideal would be for the children to share their time between both parents, but this is not always practical and takes a lot of understanding from both parents. However, it is essential for children not to lose contact with the 'absent' parent.

CONSIDERING THE NEEDS OF THE CHILDREN

Your child is basically an innocent party in a conflict that you and your partner, or both of you, have created. All children want both their parents if they have known them. You need to separate your feelings of anger and bitterness towards 'their mother' from your feelings towards your children. Their life is being turned upside down, and affected by a decision which they are not party to. They are not property, they are a part of you. They are not owned by you, they are human beings and what happens when their parents split up will affect them for the rest of their lives. You need to put your emotions on one side and ask yourself the following questions:

- What are my children's needs?

- How can their standard of living be maintained?

- Which parent is going to take day-to-day responsibility?

- How am I going to maintain them financially?

- How much contact do they need?

- What is the best way to come to an agreement with my ex-partner/mother of my children?

Changing the lifestyle of your children

Your children's lifestyle will change radically, and you must understand this consequence of the decision to split up. You must think of what really happens when finances are split. It is just as expensive to maintain a home for one as it is for a family of three. Inevitably your children are going to have to live on half of what they had before. They may also have to move home and completely uproot themselves from friends and familiar surroundings.

NEGOTIATING WITH THE OTHER PARENT

This is a very tricky subject. When you have been through a traumatic and bitter split-up, the mere thought of seeing your ex-partner is enough to drive you into a sweat. You have to decide what is best for your child. But don't forget that children have views, and even a child who has never seen their other parent will one day ask the fatal question, where is my daddy (or mummy)?

This is a very familiar question now in the UK as only 50 percent of separated/divorced fathers have any contact with their children. It is a matter of fact that a child is conceived by two parents, excluding modern technology and sperm banks, and as single parents are in the minority of family structures, your children will see two-parent families every day.

The children, usually, have not been part of your decision and lifestyle. They might have benefited but it was not their decision. You need to understand their short- and long-term needs including contact with their father and to feel loved by you. Eventually it is preferable that you are able to come to terms on a bitter-free zone, and find a way whereby the children can benefit from regular contact.

Case study: Tony is an 'absent' dad

Tony was divorced from his wife, after he had an affair with his secretary, who was ten years younger. His ex-wife, Claire, was very bitter and at first objected to Tony seeing their two boys. She told their sons, David and Martin, about his affair, and when he did call to take them out, they refused to go.

'They shouted at me and told me they hated me. I was devastated. I wrote to them that I did love them and I was sorry I had hurt them. I thought it was best to leave them alone for the time being. Then I went to a local support group for absent fathers and learnt how contact was important. I spoke to my solicitor and he persuaded Claire, through her solicitor, that we should try a local conciliation service in order to come to an agreement on the children. I knew they needed to be with their mother, but they did need to see me.

'Claire was still bitter but had realised that the boys were deeply affected by the situation and after seeing me that time when they said they hated me, they had started to blame their mother as well and the youngest started bed-wetting. It was agreed the boys would stay with me every other weekend, and I would start to take them once a week to swimming which had been a regular event since they were toddlers and which Claire could not do. Agreement on Christmas and holidays was also met.

'Claire would not initially agree for me to take the children to my new flat which I shared with my girlfriend, and it was agreed that I took them to my mother's. This did have a bad effect on my new partner and eventually she became very jealous of the children and my ex-wife. We broke up after two years. The irony was Claire remarried.

'The first few visits with the children were traumatic but my mother helped a great deal although she did not approve of what I had done. The children slowly came round to things and our love is now very strong.'

HELPING YOUR CHILDREN UNDERSTAND

Few children want their parents to split up and it is rare for a child to welcome separation. Children do not choose to have their parents separate – the decision is imposed on them. You will find it difficult and painful to cope with the breakdown of a relationship. It can be easy at this time to overlook or misunderstand your children's needs and feelings.

If you are an estranged father through a relationship ending, you will realise that splitting up is not one single event which is over and done with in a week, a month, or a year. It causes changes which continue for a long time, but this can be to your advantage as the time can be used to help your children understand and adapt to differences in their lives.

Does your child feel:
Muddled   Relieved   Fed-up   Scared   Angry?

Children rarely want their parents to separate and will go to incredible lengths to try to keep you together. They are used to the problems that cause the separation and even get used to parents storming out and not returning for several weeks, as long as they do eventually come back!

Children's fears

The point when a couple decide to separate can be confusing for all children. They seldom take part in the decision and yet they are profoundly affected by it. Children often talk of feeling like an outsider and being ignored while adults try to sort themselves out. They describe how they are left to worry about what will happen to them and how lonely they can feel. Children want you to be honest with them even if they don't fully understand.

Often children talk of being afraid that their parents will stop loving them like they stopped loving each other. Most children wonder if they are somehow to blame for the situation and are filled with guilt and regret for all the times when they have been naughty.

The child's reaction

The range of emotions a child experiences depends largely on the circumstances surrounding the separation. There is no set format and each child will react differently, but there are some general trends. Most children suddenly realise that their parents are not perfect and respect their parents less as a result. Many experience shock, either as numbness so they seem not to be affected at all, or they begin to catch every cough and cold around. Denial is common as is the feeling of betrayal, which can often lead to anger and aggression. The most destructive emotion of all is hate as it can affect a child's future relationships and cause lasting damage to their ability to function as a balanced and relaxed person.

There is a marked difference between the ways different age groups react:

- **3- to 5-year olds:** struggle to explain how they feel and seem bewildered. Many regress and return to familiar habits of thumb-sucking or clingy behaviour as a way of recapturing the security of the past. They need help to understand what has happened and reassurance that it is not their fault. They need to know about practicalities like who will look after the cat and if they can take toys with them.

- **6- to 8-year olds:** usually express real grief, crying, sobbing and sometimes even searching for their lost parents. Often their behaviour in school deteriorates. At this age, boys are particularly vulnerable and need a lot of reassurance.

- **9- to 12-year-olds:** can appear very angry and hostile, looking for someone or something to blame. They may even suffer from psychosomatic illnesses, sometimes unconsciously hoping that their illness will bring their parents back together again. Often there will be concerns from the school that the child's work and attitude are poor.

- **Teenagers:** often try to hide their mental bewilderment behind a complete refusal to see or talk to one parent. They can express their hurt through physical aggression or even vandalism as they try to distance themselves from their emotions and display an 'I don't care' attitude to their friends. Adolescents are sometimes so embarrassed that they pretend nothing has happened and even deny the separation if their friends ask about it. Truanting and general lack of co-operation can be a feature.

Why do I feel so guilty when I think of the children?
You shouldn't feel guilty for separating. You had your reasons. But remember that, although you may feel you are doing what is best for your family, your children may not feel this at all. You need to listen to them as well as getting them to listen to you.

How will my children react with only one parent?
It is not being part of a one-parent family that causes children distress, but the feelings they experience that come from having to put up with something they did not want to happen. It is important

to separate the two so as not to fall into the trap of believing that children are 'deprived' because they are from lone-parent families. Remember it is up to you as the 'absent' father to build the bridges.

Remembering the key points
- Provide honest and accurate information to your children in ways they can understand.

- Talk openly with your children so that they can make sense of what is going on.

- Give children the chance to air their feelings and their worries about both the present and the future.

- Keep the children as secure as possible and lives as unchanged as much as possible in other ways by providing the right financial support.

- Help your children keep their own identities by encouraging contact with their friends, relatives and others who care for them.

- Tell the children frequently that you love them.

- Don't let any bitterness or anger about your ex-partner affect your children's relationship with the parent they live with.

Perhaps the most important point is not to be afraid to tell your children how you feel. Many adults find it difficult to talk about feelings to their children. You may be afraid that you will lose control and the children will see you in distress. Sometimes there is a fear of losing face. Adults are supposed to be strong and able to cope. Sometimes we want to protect our children from extreme emotions as these may be too painful. However, it is important to find the right way to begin sharing your feelings with your children, so they can begin to understand what is happening for you.

CARING FOR YOUR CHILDREN AWAY FROM HOME

Just because you are not with your children on a day-to-day basis, does not mean you relinquish your responsibilities as a parent. Think carefully about your answers to the following questions:

- Why did I have children in the first place?

- How did my intentions change when my relationship ended?

- What did becoming a father do for me?

- What were my feelings for my children before and after separation?

- How has the separation affected my role and potential as a father?

Seeing your children
Short and regular visits are better than long stays with long gaps between. You need to be consistent, on time and regular. Children need the security of routine. They need your undivided attention, interest and love. Discuss with them their interests and what they would like to do. Talk and listen to them.

Remembering the key points
- Maintain contact with your children. Establish regular and frequent contact as soon as possible with as much staying contact as you can manage.

- Be determined about staying in contact with your children – it is vital for their well being. Get assistance with ways of managing this, and with advice and education on good parenting.

- Do not agree to a period of no contact. Experience shows that contact can be very difficult to re-establish after a break, and any such loss is potentially harmful to your children.

- Never let your children down. Always keep to agreed arrangements whatever happens. If the bus fails, take a taxi, whatever it costs.

- Suggest shared residence, enabling your children to share their time with both parents. This is commonplace in the USA, is known to work in almost all cases to the children's advantage, and results in high child-support compliance.

LOOKING AT THE OPTION OF SHARED PARENTING

The old saying is that two heads are better than one. It can be true for parenting if the two heads, in this case the two parents, can break the ice and find a way of communicating with each other in regard purely to the children. Remember the past is the past.

Shared parenting means that, after divorce and separation, both mother and father retain a positive parenting role in their children's lives. Sometimes it is called joint physical or joint actual custody or the newer concept of shared parental responsibility. Shared parenting is simply where the children spend substantial amounts of time with both parents. Anything from a 30/70 to a 50/50 split fits this category.

It is different from the notion of reasonable access or contact. Normally one parent has full legal custody of the child, and the other has visiting rights. All decisions on the child are made by the main 'home based' parent. In shared parenting, however, the children will normally live with one parent but regularly visit and stay with the other and both parents discuss issues regarding the children. The clear advantages of this arrangement can be as follows:

- **Financial**. The other parent will feel happy to target money to the children.

- **Support**. There is always the other parent, if illness sets in.

- **Children's feelings**. The children feel at ease with both parents and this gives a sense of balance. They are also prevented from playing one off against the other.

Case study: Martin moves towards shared parenting

After some years Martin and his ex-wife have built up a stronger relationship that enables them to discuss their children more fully. Amanda has the children during holidays and occasionally comes over for weekends so that Martin can get away.

'It was hard at first as my wife left due to illness, and all I wanted was for her to come home. When she was better she wanted to divorce and this was a painful process. Three years later I was in a second relationship which also made it difficult to bridge the gap.

'Back on my own with the kids, I started to try and make more contact, particularly as my daughter was becoming a teenager and she wanted to spend more time with her mum. I did not want her to grow into an adult with bitterness. I wanted her and my sons to know that both parents loved them very much and that even though they lived with me, they had access and contact with the other parent whenever they wished.

'For this reason we moved to be nearer to Amanda, and we are now good friends and share the mutual interest and love of our children. It has taken ten years but at least they can start their adult life knowing there are two parents who are there for them.'

FINDING SUPPORT AND ADVICE

If your relationship ends and you are separated from your children, try and make use of **Family Mediation Services**. Avoid going into an adversarial battle until all other options have been exhausted. Read the section on using conciliation and mediation services in Chapter 7.

Families Need Fathers is a national organisation for absent fathers, particularly fathers who have difficulty with gaining access to their children after divorce or relationship break-up. FNF can put you in touch with a local contact that could provide useful support and help. See Useful Addresses.

DISCUSSION POINTS

1. Think about the needs of your children and what you would like for them.

2. Find out where the nearest local conciliation service is located.

3. Contact Families Need Fathers and find out about local absent father groups.

6
Bringing Up a Child
on Your Own

There are 1.4 million single parents in the UK and 10 per cent are single parent fathers. This chapter is primarily concerned with the issue of fathers parenting on their own. However, it is important for 'absent' fathers to read this chapter to try to understand what life is like for the mothers of their children.

Bringing up your children on your own means doing practically everything. Society's general understanding is that you need two parents to bring up a child effectively. 'On your own' parenting therefore means that you have to be prepared to do two jobs in the home, and possibly three if you also go out to work. In fact many single parents have to struggle with several part-time jobs in order to carry out their home role, as they cannot fit full-time employment around the care hours. It is very hard work and should not be underestimated.

The key is to see the family as a whole unit. In fact you are not on your own, but live with your children, and as a family you develop with each other. You are the parent and in control, but your children are partners and helpers. You are on a road of adventure together. It isn't them against you.

UNDERSTANDING WHAT IT MEANS TO BE A SINGLE PARENT

'I didn't want to be a single parent. I didn't want the stigma – seems odd now! Although I knew lots of single parents, I never thought I would end up in that position. Now I'm proud to be a successful parent bringing up my children alone.'

Lone parents do face problems, mainly because our society is built around the idea that it is normal for two people to share in bringing up their children, and for one of the parents to look after them while the other goes out to earn the money. Lone parents have to do both these jobs, while living in a society that assumes that the roles will be split.

Good parenting is to do with self-esteem, being well supported and having a good and happy environment. This is true for everyone not just single parents. The more confidence you have in your parenting the more likely you will be able to cope with the ups and downs.

Facing the practical issues

Whatever the route to lone parenthood, the issues that confront lone parents are the same:

- getting your benefits and tax sorted out
- seeking payment of child maintenance
- getting a secure place to live
- sorting out the separation or divorce
- planning to go back to work
- getting childcare arrangements sorted out
- planning some leisure time and holidays.

Coping with your feelings

It is not easy being a single parent and you will go through long periods of despair. Look at the list below and see how many of these feelings you have or have had.

Hurt	Disillusioned	Lonely	Strong	Out of love
	Rejected	Nervous	Isolated	Free
Trapped	Angry	Displaced	In control	In debt
	Withdrawn	Happy	Disenchanted	Stressed
Positive	Frightened	Outcast	Special	
	Tired	Forward-looking	Hopeful	Depressed
No feelings	Numb	Joyful	Refreshed	

Case study: Martin goes it alone

Martin is bringing up his three children alone, after his wife left due to post-natal depression. He never imagined be was going to be a single parent.

'One day I was part of a two-parent, three-children family, and the next day one parent had gone. My wife just could not cope any more with bringing up three very young kids and me. She had very bad depression after Steven was born and this became worse after Mark. I tried to give support but I had a demanding job and was on a short-term contract and continually fearful I would lose my job. The fear of insecurity for my family kept me working long hours. I became blind to what was happening to my wife.

'Suddenly I was on my own and this devastated me. I just tried to keep going and as the children were young I initially kept working full-time, I had little time to think. My ex-wife started visiting regularly and we built up a good friendship that benefited us and the children.

'At one of her visits, I finally broke down in tears, it had taken nearly cight years. I loved my wife so much that I never really understood what had happened. It was like someone dying, without telling you why. I felt so alone. I always protected my children and never showed any bitterness, and made sure the children had contact with their mum. I kept them happy. Years later, my daughter told a friend that as neither I nor her mum ever explained to her what had happened, she felt guilty that it had been her fault. She blamed herself. She was only five when Amanda left. I always thought we had explained, obviously not.'

SUPPORTING THE MOTHER OF YOUR CHILDREN

It is important to note that when a father leaves his partner and children, he is creating a single parent family; that is, the burden of sole day-to-day responsibility for the care of the children falls firmly on the woman. If you accept the principle that children actively need two parents, you are automatically putting the job of two onto one. If you worked in a job that required two skilled people and one left, and you were told by your boss that you now had to do both jobs and accept a pay cut at the same time, you would be outraged and your union (if you were in one) would take immediate action. That, however, is effectively what happens when one parent leaves the family home and a single parent family is created.

This book isn't about moral judgement and it accepts that

relationships fail, but children still have two parents and in this rearrangement of the family structure, their interests must be paramount. This involves providing support for the mother who is the full-time carer.

COPING WITH PARENTING AND BEREAVEMENT

Twenty-five per cent of male single parents are widowers. In this situation you have to face the loss of the mother of your children as well as taking on full responsibility for your children.

Facing the bewilderment

No one who has not experienced the death of a partner can fully understand all its conflicting emotions. Some say it is like becoming a teenager again with all a teenager's swings of mood. You can become over-sensitive to casual remarks, dread waking up in the morning – that's if you are sleeping at all. Waking up at weekends can be a nightmare. You may speak aloud to your ex-partner, and your mind will drift away to happy times.

All these feelings are normal and there is no right way to grieve. You have to find a way through by whatever methods bring most relief and comfort. Becoming a single parent through death usually results in a wide range of support from family, friends, teachers, everyone who knows you. Many will give advice, but in the end you have to fight your own way through.

Timetable of grief

This varies and some stages overlap, but the general pattern is often along the following lines:

1. Shock

2. Numbness

3. Struggle between fantasy and reality

4. Feelings of guilt and frenzy

5. Depression

6. Release through crying

7. Painful memories

8. Acceptance.

Sharing the grief with your children

You must firstly follow your own instinct in handling your children after the death of your partner. It is a good idea not to shut children out of your grief. It is impossible to protect them completely from what has happened, but you must feel assured that they will get over it and not suffer permanent emotional damage.

There is a tendency to tell little lies initially about the death. Children are told that mummy is ill in hospital or gone away abroad. But if you don't fully tell them, eventually they will find out. Honesty is the best way.

As well as the shock and feelings of unbelief at the death of a parent, a child may be afraid of losing the other parent as well. It is important to allow your child to talk about his/her fears.

Questions to ask

- How are the children coping?

- Would they benefit from talking to a counsellor?

- Are your children's friends still coming round to play?

- Do you talk about their deceased parent?

Action to take

- Encourage them to make a special scrapbook about their parent by using photographs and pictures.

- Talk about how their parent had loved them, how you love them.

- Discuss with them what their parent would have wanted for them.

- Tell them what hopes you have for them.

- Share your hopes for the future and make plans with them.

- Be open and honest. Talk about finances and what you need to do now in building up a new life. Involve them and you will be surprised how resourceful and helpful they can be.

Finding the right support after the death of a partner

Often there is plenty of support at the time of death but this can evaporate as time goes on and you may well find yourself needing more support than you are getting from friends and family during the two years after a partner's death. Actively seek the support you need from:

- your parents
- your children
- friends
- support groups
- professional caregivers and counsellors.

Identifying a good listener
Much of the time, what you need most is someone who has the time and ability to listen to you as you talk about your concerns and problems. A good listener should be non-judgemental, able to hear the bad as well as the good and not afraid of anger.

Who do I talk to?
Your local branch of the **Citizens Advice Bureau** can supply details of local bereavement services and counsellors in your area. Your GP can also make referrals to counsellors or therapists. Even if they are not what you want they can be a good starting point.

WORKING AND CARING FOR CHILDREN

Firstly, as a full-time parent, you have a full-time job in bringing up your children. This is an important role. Be proud of that.

However, you need money to live. As a lone father, your three most likely sources of income, unless you have private savings or investments, are earned income, maintenance payments and state benefits.

The main reasons for you to work are to earn enough to live, provide for your children and improve your standard of living. Working can also be enjoyable and provide opportunities for you to develop skills and abilities. It breaks the isolation and enables you to meet others. The key is to balance all these needs with caring for your children.

The physical and emotional demands of parenting can clash with work and coping singlehanded makes this more likely. It is not necessarily easier with a partner, as most parenting usually falls to one. Many working single parents actually feel less hassled and more in control than they did when they lived with a partner and had to come home and look after them too!

It is not easy bringing up children alone as well as taking the extra strain of working. However, it is the way to more independence and it is likely that the government will develop policies that encourage more single parents this way. There are already benefits that enable you to top up your salary and assistance towards childcare costs.

FINDING THE RIGHT SUPPORT

Throughout this book, you have been advised to seek advice and support in tackling important issues in your life. As a single parent you need and have a right to support and practical help, and it is readily available from a variety of sources.

It is always a good idea to seek out sources for support and advice when in fact you don't need it, then when you do you'll know exactly where to go. The two best local sources of information on advice and support networks in your area at the **library** and the **Citizens Advice Bureau**. Both will have details of local support groups and of specialist advice whether debt counselling, housing or legal.

Gingerbread and **Span** are the two national umbrella organisations that support single parents, and they may have a contact or a local group in your area. If the nearest group is too far for you to travel, you'll find both organisations only too willing to help you link with others to form a more local group. **Gingerbread** has a national advice line which is always worth a ring. The **National Council for One Parent Families** is more a campaign organisation that provides information on all aspects of being a single parent and is constantly trying to improve the status of single parents in society. It is worth considering joining one of the above organisations purely for the positive information they provide.

There are also a range of support groups emerging for single parent fathers. See the Useful Addresses section under relevant categories.

DISCUSSION POINTS

1. Draw up a list of all the advantages and disadvantages of being on your own with the children.

2. Find out if there are any single parent support groups in your area.

3. If you are a widower, look at the grieving timetable on page 64 and work out what stage you feel you are at.

7
Knowing your Legal Rights

You may feel that as a father you have automatic legal rights over your children. However, remember that your children are not property and should not be looked at in this way. Your legal rights should not be assumed.

For instance, if you are not married to the mother of your child you have no automatic rights to your child unless your partner agrees formally or you apply through the courts. However, all fathers have the responsibility to provide maintenance for their children whether they live with them or not. No one takes much notice of the law and their rights until the day they are challenged and in the case of families this is when the parental relationship fails and ends.

It is also important to understand your legal **responsibilities** as a parent, as society is continually questioning the role of parents and their responsibility when children become out of control and break laws themselves. Already parents can be taken to court for offences committed by their children. It is very likely that legislation in the future will be more punitive of parents of wayward children.

UNDERSTANDING YOUR PARENTAL OBLIGATIONS

Parental responsibility is outlined in Chapter 1, which explains the rights and duties of parents in relation to the **Children Act 1989**.

Parents have a legal duty to care for their children properly and serious neglect of a child is a criminal offence.

There is no legal way that a child can compel his/her parents to obey the law, except that a child over 16 may be able to intervene in proceedings between his parents to ask for maintenance orders.

However, if the children are being neglected neighbours or friends can complain to the Social Services department of the local council. Social workers will visit the family, and if they think it necessary, the council may bring proceedings to put the children in care.

Parents must take care of a child when he/she is ill and ensure that he/she gets whatever medical treatment is necessary. Failure to call a doctor when one is needed or to follow their advice, or refusal to allow a blood transfusion or an operation even on religious grounds, are criminal offences like other forms of neglect, punishable by two years imprisonment and an unlimited fine.

Can my child sue me?

Yes. A parent has a duty not to harm their child through carelessness and if they do the child can sue them for compensation. For instance, if a parent carelessly causes their child, who is a passenger in their car, to be injured in an accident, the child can sue the parent and claim damages.

UNDERSTANDING THE LEGAL IMPLICATIONS

As a father you have the status and title of parent of a child or children whether married or not. As such you are affected by certain laws of the land. If you were or are in dispute with your ex-partner, whether over the custody of your children or getting legally divorced, there are laws that will determine your rights. The law also affects the bereaved father. Legislation is extremely complex but it helps to know a little and at least the title of the laws that will be used by you, through a solicitor and in the courts.

Children and parents' rights/duties

- *Child Abduction Act 1984*. Establishes criminal sanctions in relation to children taken out of British jurisdiction.

- *Children Act 1989*. Provides the framework of law for all matters relating to children including residence, contact and finances.

- *Child Support Act 1991*. Provides for a way of dealing with maintenance payments for children. Established the Child Support Agency.

Divorce and separation

- *Married Women's Property Act 1882*. Section 17 enables the court to decide on the property rights of husbands and wives.

- *Law of Property Act 1925*. Section 30 enables a cohabiting man or woman to apply for the sale of the property which he or she co-owns with his or her partner.

- *Matrimonial Causes Act 1973.* The main law for divorce (together with Family Law Act 1996, see below). Sets out how a divorce can be obtained. It explains what financial orders can be made by the court and what considerations the court will take into account in deciding financial relief issues.

- *Inheritance (Provision for the Family and Dependants) Act 1975.* Provides the law to enable a dependant to make a claim against the estate of a deceased person who does not leave reasonable provision for the claimant in his or her will.

- *Domestic Violence and Matrimonial Proceedings Act 1976.* One of the acts enabling a cohabitee/spouse to apply for injunctions ordering the ex-partner to get out of the house or stop assaulting him or her.

- *Matrimonial Homes Act 1983.* Provides a non-tenant spouse with rights of occupation and non-tenant or joint-tenant spouse with the legal right to apply to the court for a transfer of the tenancy.

- *Matrimonial and Family Proceedings Act 1984* (updated the Matrimonial Causes Act 1974). Made clean breaks more likely. Enables people divorced outside England and Wales to apply for financial relief.

- *Family Law Act 1996.* The government has reformed the divorce laws to enable married couples to divorce after eighteen months without citing either party at fault. This is a major step as the 'blame' aspect of divorce caused very acrimonious and expensive divorces. Couples are also encouraged to use mediation services.

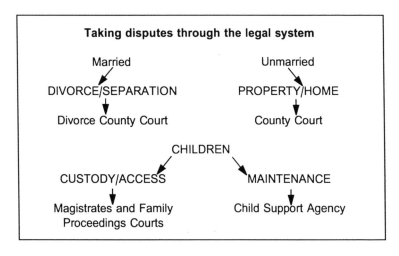

Taking disputes through the legal system

Married	Unmarried
DIVORCE/SEPARATION	PROPERTY/HOME
Divorce County Court	County Court

CHILDREN

CUSTODY/ACCESS	MAINTENANCE
Magistrates and Family Proceedings Courts	Child Support Agency

DEALING WITH DIVORCE AND CUSTODY

Your marriage has ended and you are seeking divorce and custody of your children. The formality of divorce can be very traumatic as it reduces your private life and former relationship to cold and meaningless words or pieces of paper. The law uses words that mean very little to you and often need translating into simple language. Relationships end and couples are living apart for some time before the legal process begins and there is often uncertainty about who starts what. In the majority of cases the mother is awarded custody of her children and the husband is allowed 'reasonable access'.

What are court orders?

A court order is a form of judgement that states what will happen to your child. There are four main orders:

- **Residence Order** – details on who your child will live with.

- **Contact Order** – details the allowed contact of the other parent.

- **Specific Issue Order or Prohibited Steps Order** – this allows one parent to prevent the custodial parent from doing things they object to, e.g. moving abroad or changing their name.

- **Family Assistance Order** – this is not very common, but it allows the court to appoint a social worker or another family member to advise on the upbringing of the child. Could be used for teenage mums.

USING CONCILIATION AND MEDIATION

'Mediation' and 'conciliation' are both terms used to refer to a range of means of coming to an agreement with your ex-partner about the arrangements of splitting up. The process involves using an independent mediator. Hopefully it takes some of the unhelpful negative emotion out of the situation and enables you to get down to practicalities. The central and important question is the welfare of the children.

Mediation is done by discussion and negotiation and is available to married and unmarried couples. One or two trained workers sit with you and try to help the discussion keep to practical issues. The priority issues are concerned with the children, but some services also help with financial negotiations.

Using mediation can be far better than trying to resolve issues through the courts. It is also cheaper as the service is usually charged by the hour and most mediation services work out their fee according to your ability to pay.

Can I use this service without the co-operation of my ex?

Yes. You go along and talk over the issues that need to be resolved. The service will write to your partner and ask them to come and initially talk to them on their own. When they have an agreement to co-operate with the process, they will bring both parties together.

How do I find a Conciliation Service?

There are services all around the country, and following revision of the divorce laws, further services are planned. Your solicitor, local county court and Citizens Advice Bureau will have details. The main national mediation services are listed at the back of this book.

ACKNOWLEDGING THE LEGAL RIGHTS OF THE OTHER PARENT

Whether you have been married or not, the legal position of the children is of prime importance. You need to know your legal rights to your children and the rights of the other parent, as it is this that can cause bitter disputes and result in battles for legal custody. **The Children Act 1989** is the main law which protects the interests of your child. The Act defines who has the right to be the legal parent of your child and which parent has the full responsibility.

All mothers and married fathers have automatic legal rights to their children and have legal responsibility for them. Unmarried fathers do not have an automatic right although under the **Child Support Act**, they have a duty to maintain the child.

What situations give rise to legal disputes about children?

- You have been married and are now divorcing.

- You have been living with your child's other parent and the relationship has ended.

- You have never lived together with your child's other parent and cannot agree arrangements between yourselves, e.g. the unmarried father wants to see his child.

- Other people have concerns about the children and wish either to have access to them or to take them into their care. This could include grandparents, a former foster parent, or the local Social Services Department. If you are concerned about your children being put into care, you need urgently to seek detailed advice and you should contact your local Citizens Advice Bureau or law centre.

I am an unmarried father: can I get legal rights of responsibility to my child?
Yes. There are several ways. Either the mother makes a Parental Responsibility agreement with the father, or the father applies to the court for a Parental Responsibility Order. This can be complex as the father has to prove he is the other parent and put up a very strong case that it is in the best interest of the child. This often arises when the mother has left the child in the care of the unmarried father and the school or local Social Services have questioned his legal rights to the child.

What happens if I have a maintenance order against me, but am denied access?
A father must pay maintenance for his child, but if you want to have access you have to apply separately to the courts for a contact order. Maintenance is dealt with separately by the Child Support Agency. Your ex-partner has the right to object to your application.

PROVIDING MAINTENANCE

As a parent you have a legal obligation to feed, clothe and properly provide for your children according to your family's standard of living. Neglect is a criminal offence. When a father or mother leaves the home and their children, he/she still has a legal obligation to provide financial maintenance. The remaining parent can bring an application for an order for maintenance against the father or mother if she/he believes that there is failure to provide reasonable maintenance for their children. However, since 1991, most applications for maintenance are dealt with by the Child Support Agency.

Child Support Agency
All questions involving regular payments for the maintenance of children, whether you have been married or not, are dealt with by the Agency. The agency was established under the Child Support Act 1991. In simple terms, the Act states that all parents must contribute financially to the upbringing of their children. If the

remaining parent with the children receives benefit from the state, they will have to provide details of the 'absent' father or mother of the children, and the CSA will pursue them for payment.

FIGHTING FOR ACCESS

Providing maintenance does not guarantee access to your children. This has to be applied for through the courts. The issue of the children is primarily dealt with through the divorce process and in most cases the courts will make an order that you have 'reasonable access'. However, what the judge defines as reasonable might be not very reasonable to you. Also your ex-wife might have a different interpretation. Although access is not linked to maintenance, your ex-wife could see failing to keep up maintenance payments as a signal to stop access. Your ex-wife could also put up a strong case that it is not in the interests of the children for you to have access. It is not in the interests of the child to get in between parents in an acrimonious dispute, but he/she does need the love of both his/her parents and this means contact. If you have to fight for access and have tried all the conciliatory routes but have failed to reach an agreement, you will have to go to court.

Remembering the key points
- Beware of totally undefended divorce. The allegations made may be used against you in later proceedings, thereby affecting contact, residence and finance.

- Think carefully before leaving the matrimonial home. You may never get back even to see your children.

- Press your lawyer. Insist they carry out your instructions. Ensure they act in good time, and provide them with or follow up with written instructions.

- Think about conducting your own case. You are entitled to have a friend alongside you in court.

- Consider calling expert witnesses. The judge may not share your views on what is best for your children.

- Be wary of 'reasonable contact'. Your partner may not agree with you about what is 'reasonable'. Insist upon 'defined contact' and prepare a detailed plan which is, and can be seen to be, in the best interests of your children.

- If the court appoints a welfare officer, ensure that it gives appropriate directions about the matters to be investigated, and also orders that your children are seen with each parent (and the new partners) in their respective home(s).

- If your welfare report is unfavourable or contains inaccuracies, ask for it to be amended or for a new welfare report. Be prepared to appeal.

- Do not agree to your children going into care. It may be very difficult to get them out again. Never give up. However difficult it is, you must keep trying.

I am not married: can I get access to my children?

The mother of your children has total rights over them, unless you have made a proper agreement for shared legal responsibility. If she denies you access, you will have to go to court and apply for a contact order.

FINDING THE RIGHT LEGAL ADVICE

We all need advice and particularly advice on anything we find difficult to understand. To know your rights you need to know where to ask the questions and what questions to ask.

Where do I get legal advice?

- Solicitor.
- Local law centre.

The main source of legal advice and assistance is solicitors, but it is often best to start with organisations that specialise in general or specific advice.

What can a solicitor do for me?

A solicitor advises you about the law, and helps you decide the best course of action. They can act as an effective emotional screen between you and your ex-partner and hopefully reduce the areas of conflict between you.

How do I find a suitable solicitor?

You need to find a solicitor who has relevant experience in the law you need advice on. For example, if you are seeking a divorce or need to fight for access to your children, you need a solicitor with experience of Family Law. Ask around to a variety of sources and see if the same name comes up several times.

Sources of help in finding a solicitor
- Ask **family** and **friends**. Have they had good experiences with a local solicitor?

- Ask local **Families Need Fathers** groups and other divorced/ estranged fathers.

- Consult the **Solicitors Regional Directory** at your local library or Citizens Advice Bureau.

- Send a stamped addressed envelope to the **Solicitors Family Law Association**.

How do I make sure I am getting a good solicitor?
Ask questions. All solicitors will usually give the first appointment free and you should use this to find out whether he/she is suitable for you. Often the personality, sex and age of the solicitor will be an important factor. You might feel more at home with an older man, or a woman.

CONTROLLING THE LEGAL PROCESS

It is your life that is being put through the legal wringer, and it is important for you to make sure that you keep control. Don't forget the reasons why you are going to court:

- to legally untangle your relationship

- to resolve who gets the children.

Remember the key points
- Be clear in your own mind about what you want.

- Ask questions.

- Get second opinions and advice from support organisations.

- Ask about costs.

- Find the best and least conflicting route.

WRITING A WILL

- Do you have a will?

- Do you have a will but have not changed it since you left?

It is hard to think the unthinkable, but something could happen to you and without a will, your children's welfare could be endangered more than necessary. You need to identify clearly, the person who will act as the guardian of your children in the event of your death. You may be happy for them to be cared for by the other parent; on the other hand, you may not. Or you may be a widow/widower yourself and not have any other relatives. It is hard to imagine, but you need to find someone who is willing to take this responsibility and carry out your wishes.

How will my children live financially?
If you are in work it is good idea to consider a life insurance policy, with the children as the named beneficiaries.

Do I have to pay a solicitor to write a will?
No, but it is still a good idea to consult a solicitor. You can write one yourself, but you should at least seek advice about possible pitfalls – at the least by speaking to friends or consulting books.

DISCUSSION POINTS

1. Consider your legal obligations towards your child and whether you fully take parental responsibility. Discuss this with the mother of your child.

2. Seek out suitable legal advice, and draw up a set of questions about your legal concerns.

3. Consider the issue of care for the children in the event of your death. Think about writing a will.

8
Understanding the Financial Needs of Children

Children do cost, and having a family will change your entire financial structure. They are mini-versions of you and need all the same things from clothing to food, from toys to a home, as well as the added costs of childcare and education.

The cost of children		
Clothes 0–18	Transport – family car to pram to bicycles	Food
Accommodation (larger home)	Toys	Education (school meals to college fees)
Holidays	Childcare (pre-school nursery to nanny)	Pocket money
Leisure activities		Health and hygiene

REALISING YOUR FINANCIAL RESPONSIBILITY

Once your child is born you have a financial responsibility to that child until it becomes of age. This is law and is outlined in the **Child Support Act 1991**. This applies to all parents whether married or unmarried. If you leave your children, the remaining parent has a right to pursue you with the aid of the **Child Support Agency** to make sure you provide reasonable maintenance. If your ex-partner and children end up on state benefit, the CSA will pursue you as the absent parent to reclaim money that it has provided towards the care of your children. You can go underground but you will be pursued. In a divorce situation, a parent receiving income support has to provide details of the absent parent and could have their benefit reduced if they don't provide this information.

Even though you have a legal responsibility to provide for your children, it is assumed that as a responsible father you will want your children to grow up healthy and with the best possible advantages.

UNDERSTANDING THE COSTS OF CHILDHOOD

Everything you need to care for your family has a financial cost and you need to continually revalue your expenditure as prices rise. Most mothers become experts in finding bargains, collecting money-off vouchers and buying from car boot sales. Discuss with her the weekly expenditure. Many relationships split up simply because couples are not able to communicate openly about money which leads to depression and arguments.

Look at this list, and add to it what you have paid out this year on these items.

Items   £

Food...

Clothes...

Holidays ....

Childcare equipment: e.g. pram, buggy, playpen.....................

Furniture: e.g. bunkbeds, bed, bookcases, fun wallpaper ....

Transport: e.g. family car with car seat/child safety locks,
        bicycle...

Health..

TOTAL..

UNDERSTANDING YOUR FINANCES

The important thing for you is that you must come to terms with your finances if you want to get in control of your life. You will be amazed by what you can achieve when you start to understand your money. Many fathers bottle up their financial worries and this leads to arguments and relationships getting into difficulty.

Here is a starter checklist to get you on the road to better control.

• Face up to your finances. Write down your income against your expenditure. See the sample sheet on page 80. Be absolutely honest!

• Do you owe money? Write a list of all you owe and to whom.

• If in debt, try to establish how you got into debt in the first place.

Income	At the moment	In the future
Earnings		
Child Benefit		
One Parent Benefit		
Maintenance		
Income Support		
Family Credit		
Housing Benefit		
Council Tax Benefit		
Any other income/benefit		
TOTAL INCOME		
Expenditure		
Rent/mortgage		
Food		
Council Tax		
Electricity		
Gas		
Other fuel costs		
Childcare costs		
Travel		
Clothes		
School meals		
Work expenses		
Newspapers/cigarettes		
Social life		
Debts		
Any other expenses		
TOTAL EXPENDITURE		

- Identify the essential debts/payments.

- Keep companies that you owe money to informed of any problems in meeting repayments.

- Talk to your partner/mother of your children.

- Go and talk to a money adviser or your bank manager, taking all the relevant information. Talking about your financial situation starts to enable you to understand it. It is not a social stigma any more to have financial problems.

Writing a child-centred income & expenditure checklist
Keeping a list of your expenditure and income sounds tedious. However, unless you have some idea of how much you are spending and on what, it is difficult to decide where you can cut down, and what you can really afford to pay on debts. Are you spending enough on the right things? Use the checklist on page 80 to help you assess your financial situation.

Claiming all your benefit entitlements
It is essential that you claim every state benefit that you are entitled to. You may be in a well-paid job and think you are not entitled to benefits, but don't take this for granted. Seek advice either from the **Benefits Agency** or from your local **Citizens Advice Bureau**. For example, you may have a low income and be eligible for Family Credit, housing and council tax benefit. Your children may be entitled to free school meals. You need to check all these out. All families with children are entitled to Child Benefit, plus One Parent Benefit if one parent leaves or dies.

PAYING AND CLAIMING MAINTENANCE

As a father you have a legal obligation to provide for your children, and in the event of you leaving your children you will have to provide financial maintenance.

Maintenance normally involves regular payments from a parent who is no longer living with the children to help towards paying for their everyday needs.

Previously, maintenance arrangements were dealt with solely by the courts. Since April 1993 there has been a new system for arranging child maintenance which is directed under the Child Support Act.

The **Child Support Agency** (CSA), which is a section of the Department of Social Security, assesses, collects and enforces the payment of child maintenance. You still use the courts if you need to claim maintenance for yourself as the CSA only targets maintenance for children.

How is the maintenance calculated?
There is a formula for calculating maintenance which takes into account the individual circumstances of the family and the absent parent. These include:

- The day-to-day living expenses of the person with care and the children for whom the assessment is being made, together with housing costs.

- The day-to-day living expenses of the absent parent and any 'natural' children (i.e. children by birth or adoption but not stepchildren) living with them, together with housing costs.

- The net income of the absent parent and parent with care.

Both parents are responsible for supporting their children.

How is the money paid?
It can be paid directly, via the CSA or via the courts.

CONTROLLING YOUR MONEY

It is not easy to control your money, but it is possible and, more importantly, you will get great satisfaction in winning control. Parenthood is often filled with a lot of guilt and many of us spend lavishly on our children when we cannot afford to do so. It is important to remember that your children need you not the gifts you can buy.

Do you remember the time when you gave your child a toy in a big box and she preferred the box? Great enjoyment can be had from making toys, cooking special economy meals and freezing them, walks out in the park as opposed to visits to the cinema.

Though don't forget that many cinemas have children's clubs offering cheaper tickets at certain times.

Don't hide things from the children. Make them part of the exercise. You will be surprised what savings ideas they have. They may want to hire a video. Great! Why not explore the video hire at your local library, often half the price? The key to controlling your money is do not rush into things, take time, think about it, talk to people/advice agencies, write down a list of essential expenditure and possible savings.

Remembering the key points

- Budget to save something each month, however little.

- Harden up. Decide what you really need to have a reasonable lifestyle.

- When you go out, take just enough cash to cover your purchases.

- Make a note of everything you buy, and the price. Encourage your children to do the same.

- Avoid 'buy now, pay later' signs.

- If you have credit cards, put them away for real emergencies, or get rid of them.

- If you have to borrow, always check the APR (annual percentage rate). The lower the rate, the less interest you pay. Look for interest-free arrangements.

DISCUSSION POINTS

1. Check whether you are receiving all your benefit entitlements. Make an appointment with the Benefit Agency or Citizens Advice Bureau.

2. Draw up an income and expenditure chart and debt list.

3. Regularly discuss finances with your partner.

9
Coping with the Stress
of Being a Father

Each year six million people consult their doctor because they feel depressed or anxious. It is quite normal, and fathers do not live in a stress-free zone.

As a father you are not living in a stress-free zone. Being a parent is very stressful in itself, and balancing this with meeting the needs of your partner and of work can at times seem impossible. If your relationship ends and you have to take up the role of 'absent' father, you will go through the total trauma of relationship breakdown and the need to establish a new relationship with your children that may mean only seeing them once a week. Or you may be a single-parent father taking the full burden of parental responsibility, which is like taking on the stress levels of two people.

There is no easy solution. Even finding a new partner and creating a new stepfamily situation does not ease it. The high failure rate in second relationships shows that starting afresh can be just as stressful. However, this book is not about doom and gloom, it is about finding positive ways that will help you come to terms with your situation, turning negative situations into positive ones. The aim is to provide ideas and suggestions on how to make your life more rewarding and happy, and that means getting your stress levels down.

Surveys show that financial difficulties, work, illness, unemployment, children and personal relationships are the top six factors most responsible for stress. Fathers sometimes face all six, and can find it extremely difficult to express their distress and share these worries with others.

TAKING APPROPRIATE ACTION

Some people thrive on stress, some deal with it very successfully. But what happens when your life becomes more and more stressful so that you feel unable to cope? You need to take action, because stress builds up and can lead to physical ailments and illness.

Too much stress in your life often leads to headaches, insomnia, depression, irritability, tiredness and lower resistance to infections – colds, flu and cold sores are prime examples. The problem with stress is that many people try to combat it by turning to alcohol, coffee and tea, cigarettes, bingeing or not eating, and drugs both prescribed and illegal. While some of these might offer temporary relief, they actually make the situation worse.

TALKING WITH THE MOTHER OF YOUR CHILD

There is often much discussion about whether men can express their feelings. Women often have networks of friends with whom they can express and share problems. It is debatable whether men have similar networks. It is often thought that men get much of their emotional energy from work, whereas women tend to get their emotional energy from the family and home.

It is often difficult for men to express themselves and show vulnerability and weakness. The image of man has traditionally been about being the breadwinner and protector of his female mate and children. It is hard to admit that you are having great difficulty in achieving this ideal.

It is important to talk and share, and the most important person to communicate with is your partner and the mother of your child.

TALKING TO YOUR CHILDREN

We all need to talk and we need friends. Do not overlook the fact that friends are there with you in your home. Yes, your children. They are there when you are pulling your hair out. They see the stress, and even if they are very young, they do have concerns for you as they love you. You are their father. Your healthy existence is extremely important to them, and a stressed-out and deeply depressed parent is going to worry them, make them react in a variety of ways that could cause more stress for you. See them as a positive source of support. It is not a question of them against you, although it seems that way at times. Talk to them, tell them the truth about why you are stressed, get them on your side and positively working with you not against you.

PLANNING YOUR LIFE

What you have to do is get down to the root causes, if you can, and also find ways of relieving the symptoms and helping yourself to cope.

To begin with, examine the areas of your life that are most stressful and try to work out some solutions and alternatives. For example, the simple problem of not being able to find your keys as you are leaving the house causes your stress levels to rise – you are made late by searching for them. But situations can be resolved. It is in your power to do so.

Don't be overwhelmed by what you have to do. Make lists and break jobs down into stages. It's quite a good idea to have daily, weekly and monthly plans for what you want to achieve. But don't set yourself impossible goals and be prepared to be flexible. Ticking items off your plans as you go along brings a sense of achievement and you will feel much more in control.

GETTING THE CHILDREN TO WORK WITH YOU

You have a child or children who are part of your team. They may fight, argue, stamp their feet, and at times make your life a misery. But they are yours and your team. Get them to work with you. Simple chores around the home can be made fun and children like doing things. Yes, they might not do things the way you want them and not as efficiently, but they have to learn. Think about what your mum or dad did with you. How did you help?

TALKING WITH OTHERS

Stress is often caused because you bottle it up. You hide it from yourself and others. You become afraid to talk about your problems.

Always remember that what you are feeling is being felt by thousands of others, and a problem shared is a problem spared. The simple act of talking honestly and openly about your situation, its up and downs, can be a great relief. It often has the effect of putting everything into perspective, especially when friends say how they are feeling the same and tell you how they overcame the problem. It is a cliché but nevertheless true that there is always someone worse off than yourself.

Who do I talk to?
Wife, partner, relatives, friends, your local doctor (who can refer you for counselling), advice lines and parent support groups.

GETTING SUPPORT IN A CRISIS

Realising you need support in a crisis normally occurs to you only when you're in the middle of one. Your job may be going wrong and you are not getting home till late, or your children may be ill and you and your partner both have to go to work. You might just be at the end of your tether and need to talk to someone.

You should always talk to your partner, but sometimes you will need to talk to others too.

There are a range of local support contacts such as your doctor, or the local social services, as well as national support organisations that can advise on solutions. It is a case of building a network of support so that when something goes wrong, you know you can call on someone.

DEVELOPING SUPPORT NETWORKS

You need support sometimes, and it is a good idea to develop your own and link into existing networks.

Develop your own group by asking friends (other fathers) around to your home to discuss each others' problems and how you can help each other. **Families Need Fathers** have groups all round the UK.

Parent Support Groups

Bringing up children is one of the hardest jobs you will face. Parents are just expected to know how to cope, so it is hardly surprising that there are times when you need help and advice before you feel able to carry on. Many groups offer support, advice and counselling for parents via a telephone helpline and a range of written advice. They are sometimes staffed by professionals from a variety of backgrounds who can help find reasonable solutions for family problems.

DISCUSSION POINTS

1. Write down a list of things you like doing and plan a week where you include at least one hour of activity a day which you do on your own.

2. Write a list of all the contact numbers you need in a crisis, including friends, the school, doctor, parents, dentist, local parent support group, Parentline and Families Need Fathers. Put the list up somewhere so that you can see it in an emergency.

3. Find out about all the local support groups that are relevant to you. Ask your local Citizens Advice Bureau and library.

10
Working and Caring for Children

The traditional role of the father has been the breadwinner and protector, whereas the mother would be the carer and nurturer of the children and homemaker. This role was enshrined in law eighty years ago by the fact that women totally depended on men, who alone had the vote and the rights to ownership of property. The situation has now radically changed. Men and women are equal and the roles are not as crystal clear. Each couple and family has to evolve their own understandings of the different roles.

Many families rely totally on the father and mother both earning income, combined with sharing the domestic and childcare roles. Many women are the only partner working, with the father being the main homemaker. Women are asking their male partners to play a more active part in the family and men themselves want to take part.

The traditional split of responsibility (men at work, women at home) was easy to understand. Most employment is not family friendly and working hours are not usually flexible. Although this is changing, it is still not easy to combine an active role in the family and work. Women have been trying this balancing act for many years and will tell you how stressful it is, and how unsympathetic many male employers can be when you ring in and say you will be late as you have to take a sick child to the doctor.

You have to decide your priorities and work towards balancing the financial needs of your family and children with their and your emotional needs.

UNDERSTANDING THE JOB OF BEING A MOTHER

Being a parent is a job, a vocational and loving job, but a job. A famous politician once said that it was harder being a father than a politician. Being a full-time parent and homemaker is not an easy option and paid work is often much easier. The parent at home with the children is often isolated and having to self-motivate themselves as well as being the chief motivator of the children. The job of day-to-day parent is wide ranging, from simple domestic chores to being a nurse, from entertainer to cook to educator.

You need to understand and value what your partner does and take an interest. Find out what is going on. You may be the main provider financially but you are not necessarily doing the hardest job.

EQUALITY IN THE HOME

A father has an important role in promoting equality of the sexes. A son sees his father as his primary male role model and his attitudes to women will be developed from yours. The kind of father he eventually becomes will be determined how he sees you in that role. A daughter has a romantic attachment to her father which affects how she will see men in the future. How her mother interacts with her father and her mother's role in the family will have an effect on her aspirations. Men and women want a greater equality and wish to develop a more equal partnership. This will have a great effect on how your children will develop into adults.

In the last week, who did what around the home? Complete the checklist on page 90 and see how many of the everyday chores you, your partner or your children undertook.

SHARING THE CHORES

This is not just a case of sharing chores between you and your partner. The children should also be involved. Even very young children can do simple chores and the old saying 'start them young' is very appropriate.

Talk about the chores. Find out what your partner hates doing and what you like. Agree the priorities, which are not the same as what you like or dislike doing.

Case study: Carlton shares the housework

'We came to an early arrangement in our relationship about how we liked to organise our lives and who was better at certain things and who hated what etc. I find ironing difficult. Dawn is quite happy to iron but hates cooking. I love cooking and find it relaxing. So I do most of the cooking and Dawn does the laundry. As a family we have a rota for the washing up which we all hate. This does cause arguments as everyone tries to get out of it, and I'm happy to leave it to pile up whereas Dawn wants it done and cleared away. The

	Mum	Dad	Children
Cooking/meals			
Breakfast			
Lunch			
Tea			
Dinner			
Washing up after meals			
Cleaning			
Toilets			
Kitchen surfaces and floor			
Oven			
Living room			
Bedrooms			
Bathroom			
Windows			
Laundry			
Wash own clothes			
Wash all family clothes			
Wash curtains			
Ironing			
Children			
Feed them			
Take them to school			
Pick them up			
Bathe them			
Help them get dressed			
Read to them			

shopping we take in turns but do discuss what we need for the week and preferences. This we started to do when Dawn would be careful on her shopping visits and on mine I would come back with the expensive products, like the adverts. But now we take turns and agree a list.'

BALANCING YOUR HOME LIFE WITH WORK

It all depends on the job you have and your own personal priorities. Whatever you do, a happy home life is important for a balanced and high quality life, plus your children and partner should be either your first priority in life or at least equal with your career. This may seem a harsh statement but it is a fact that if you make your children feel secondary to your working life you will find they will grow up with deep resentment. It is possible to be a Prime Minister and an active father – it would be very hard work and you would need to develop a strong sense of priorities.

Think of your family's needs and your work needs and find ways that can bring balance. This may, for example, mean working late to finish off a piece of work in preference to taking it home. At least when you are home you will be able to give your family your full attention.

DISCUSSION POINTS

1. Take the household duty checklist and find out who does what. Add to it, and discuss the results with the family.

2. Discuss with people at work whether your hours are family friendly. Could flexible working practices be introduced?

3. Contact Parents at Work (see Useful Addresses) and find out about companies that have family-orientated work practices.

11
Choosing Good Childcare
and Schooling

As parents you will have to find others to help you educate your children, including pre-school and school.

KNOWING YOUR RIGHTS

The choice of school your child will attend is a vital one. New legislation has strengthened your rights to have a say in your children's education. Your rights are to:

- get a place in the school you choose for your children, unless there are good reasons against this
- receive information about what is taught in the school, including sex education and entry to public examinations
- elect parent governors forming a quarter of the governing body
- receive an annual report on what the governors and the school achieved in the past year. See page 98 on selecting a school.

THE NEED FOR GOOD CHILDCARE

A primary need for all parents is good, local and inexpensive childcare. The reality is that in most areas childcare provision is limited and expensive with inflexible hours. However, there is a slow growth and the government (local and national) and the private sector are recognising the need for good childcare if skilled parents are to be encouraged to return to work and/or to remain in employment.

The options for childcare are the use of your support network (family and friends), voluntary sector provision such as playgroups and after-school clubs, paid childminders, or private or state nurseries.

Finding good childcare is important because it allows you and your partner the flexibility of continuing in work, getting a job, seeking further education or giving time to yourself.

USING FRIENDS AND FAMILY

It can be the ideal solution if a close friend or relative lives locally and is willing to help. But remember that informal arrangements like these can have their own problems. A relative may feel they cannot say no and over a period of time may feel put upon, especially if there is no payment involved.

FINDING OUT ABOUT LOCAL CHILDCARE PROVISION

Following the Children Act 1989, Social Services have a duty to register daycare provision for children under eight, including childminders, while taking children up to the age of 14 into consideration. Provision has been extended to include crèches and out-of-school care, with a review every three years. It varies, obviously, according to different authorities, though most of them respond very swiftly to initial enquiries.

Step One: find out what is available in your area.
- *Yellow Pages* lists local groups under 'Crèche Facilities and Services', 'Day Nurseries' and 'Nursery Schools'.

- The local education office (number from the *Phone Book* or library) should provide a list of state nursery schools.

- Local Social Services (Early Years Section) should provide a list of all childminders, local playgroups and nurseries.

- Local libraries hold lists of groups, but you can't take the library list away with you!

- Your local school may tell you which groups most of their children come from. This can be useful if you know that your child will be going to the local school at age five.

Step Two: personal arrangements
Once you know all the types of childcare in your area, you should consider:

1. How many days and which days would be the most convenient for you and your child?

Name of group   **Date of Visit**

1. Did you like the atmosphere of the group?   Yes/No

2. Did the children seem happy?   Yes/No

3. Were they well supervised?   Yes/No

4. Did they have a good range of activities?   Yes/No

5. Would your child/children feel comfortable there?   Yes/No

6. Can you afford the costs?   Yes/No

7. Can your child have the sessions you want?   Yes/No

8. Are you totally happy with the group?   Yes/No

If you have 6 or more 'Yes' answers you should visit again taking your child with you. Watch his or her reaction and fill in the final section of the checklist

9. Did your child enjoy the visit?   Yes/No

10. Did he/she seem relaxed in the group/
    with the childminder?   Yes/No

11. Did the staff ask his/her name?   Yes/No

12. Did you still like the group on this visit?   Yes/No

Other comments:

2. Would you prefer mornings or afternoons or both?

3. What are the costs of the sessions and of travel to and from the group?

Draw up a short list of three or four options which you think you would like to explore further.

Step Three: knowing what to look for when you visit

*   Make an informal visit first and notice what the group/ childminder is like when they are not expecting you! Note your initial impression, e.g. do they make you feel welcome? Do the children seem happy?

*   If you like the group/childminder, arrange to return for a proper visit. Ask if they have any written information and are registered with the local authority.

*   Try to make your main visit without your child so you are free to watch and listen without distraction. Arrive early to watch the children arriving and notice how they greet the staff/childminder. Are they pleased to be there?

*   Ask if you can stay to watch quietly on your own for a few minutes. A good group/childminder should welcome this, but badly run childcare facilities can rarely keep the children happily occupied for long without problems showing, particularly if they only expected you to stay for half an hour.

Step Four: making your decision

A particularly charming childminder or playgroup leader can leave you with good impressions, but try filling in the checklist on page 94 after you have visited.

Step five: checking that you made the right choice

After 4 to 6 weeks settling in, your child should look forward to going and talk about what they have done. That is the best indicator that you have made the right choice!

CONSIDERING THE BEST ALTERNATIVES

There are a range of options for you when it comes to choosing the best form of childcare for you and your child's needs. The table on pages 96–97 is a useful guide that will help explore all the options.

A Guide to Childcare

Key points	Type of childcare		
	Family and friends	Childminder	Mother's help
One person looking after your child	Yes	Yes	Yes
Staff/child ratio	1:1	1:3/4	1:1
Age range	Any age	0–5	Any age
Consistency of childcare	Probably	Long-term care	Tend to move on quite soon
Other children being cared for alongside	Family usually no. Friends often have their own children too	Yes – ages mixed	No
Educational activities	Possibly	Possibly	Possibly
Training/experience	Usually experience only	Usually experience only	Little
Must be registered with local authority	No	Yes	No
Childcare in own home	Possibly	No	Yes
Have to take the child	Possibly	Yes	No
Have to pick child up on time	Possibly	Yes	Less so if they live in
Help in your home	Possibly	No	Housework
Hours shorter than usual working day/ will need supplementing	No	No	No
Problems when you child is ill	Possibly	Probably if she cares for other children	Possibly inexperienced to look after
Problems when you are ill	Probably not	Getting child there	No
Problems when you child carer is ill	Yes	Yes	Yes
Care for children of school age after school	Yes	Possibly	Yes
Holidays – cover school holidays	Yes	Yes	Yes
You can specify to your own child's needs	Yes	Possibly	Yes
Flexible hours to suit your particular needs	Possibly	Possibly	Yes
Cost	Low cost or pay in kind	Varies	Varies
Where do you find childcare	Through asking	List from local authority	Advertise/ agency

Nanny	Au pair	Day nursery	Workplace nursery/crèche	Playgroup nursery class	After school club
Yes	Yes	No	No	No	No
1:1	1:1	1:8 (3–5) 1:3 (0–2)	1:8	1:8	1:8
Any age	Any age	6 mths – 5	2–5	3–5	5–15
Varies	Turnover high	Turnover of staff may be high	Turnover of staff may be high	Likely	Likely
No but you could share with another family	No	Yes	Yes	Yes	Yes
Possibly	Unlikely	Probably	Probably	Yes	Usually no
Usually trained, experience varies	No	Yes	Yes	Yes	At least half the staff
No	No	Yes	Yes	Yes	Usually, but not statutory
Yes	Yes	No	No	No	No
No	No	Yes	Yes	Yes	Normally will collect from school
Less so if they live in	Less so	Yes	Yes	Yes	Yes
Child-related home duties	Housework	No	No	No	No
No	Yes for pre-school children	No	No	Yes	Yes 3 pm – 6pm except holidays – normal working day
No	Inexperienced and hours too short	Not applicable, as child will not attend if ill			
No	No	You need to get children there and collected, need help at home			
Possibly	Possibly	No	No	No	No
Yes	Yes	No	No	No	Yes
Yes	Yes	If private open all year; state nursery closed in holidays	May have fixed holidays	Same as school term	Usually special school holiday playscheme
Yes	Yes	No	No	No	No
Yes	Yes (may need to go to college)	No	No	No	No
Varies	Board plus a min. of £35 pw.	Varies	Varies	Varies	Varies
Advertise, Lady magazine	Au pair agency	List from local authority, Yellow Pages	Employer, trade union	List from local authority	School list from local authority, education authority, Kids Club Network

SELECTING A SCHOOL

All children have to go to school by the age of five, although many start at four these days. As a parent you not only want your child to go to school but you have a legal obligation to send them or provide an equivalent education. Finding the right school for your child is essential if he or she is to find his/her true potential.

Schooling is usually split into three stages: infant, junior and secondary. Infant and junior schools are often combined into primary schools. Transfer to secondary education is usually at age 11. However, some local authorities opt for 'middle schools' for children aged 9–13 (Years 5–8).

The majority of children go to state schools which are paid for through your taxes. All children in the UK have a right to free education. If you wish to send your child to private schools then you will have to pay. The government has introduced a voucher scheme for children aged 4–5, that enables you to use either state or private day nurseries prior to full-time education. This is part of the government's policy to widen parental choice. Whether you use state or private schools, you need to ask the right questions.

Questions to ask at primary school

1. What are the arrangements for children to visit before starting?

2. If four-year-olds are admitted, are there any extra non-teaching staff in their classes, as there would be in a nursery class?

3. How big are the classes, and are they smaller for the youngest children?

4. What are the arrangements for settling children in during their first few weeks?

5. Is any special help given to summer-born children who are often late starters and can fall behind?

6. How are the teaching groups arranged? Not all primary schools teach in year groups, with all the five-year-olds together, and so on. Arrangements should be stable.

7. How long does a single teacher stay with one class? And do the older children work at all with specialist teachers? Continuity is important to young children.

8. Does the school provide parents with details of its curriculum, reading schemes, etc.?

9. Are parents expected to work with the teacher in a formal way, reading at home with children, for instance? Home–school co-operation in this way has been shown to be most helpful for children's learning.

10. Does the school put a high priority on children's creative as well as academic work? Look at the displays around the school for an answer!

11. How are the children prepared for their move to their next school?

Questions to ask at secondary school

1. How are children introduced to the school in the first week or so?

2. Are the younger children treated in any way differently from the older ones: by being taught in a separate building, for instance, or by playing in a more protected area? Eleven-year-olds can find their new secondary school a bit overwhelming.

3. How is the school organised in terms of classes, teaching groups, houses, sixth-form accommodation, etc.?

4. Who is the person mainly responsible for the welfare of the individual child? One person (at least) should know your child well.

5. How does the school report back to parents on progress or if there are problems?

6. How does it make arrangements for particularly slow learners? And for the particularly gifted child?

7. How do the older students treat the younger children? Bullying should not be tolerated.

8. What is the school's policy on homework? It should have one.

9. Is a check made on whether homework is not only done but also marked regularly?

10. What are the arrangements for choice of exam subjects, careers education, and transfer to the sixth form, local colleges or higher education?

Questions to ask at all schools

1. How does the school organise its teaching: by ability, by age, or in some other sort of group? What is crucial is not the system but the staff's commitment to it.

2. What are the school's rules and the sanctions on uniform, discipline, etc.? Rewards are more effective than punishments.

3. If teaching is organised in ability groups, how are transfers made for children who are wrongly placed?

4. How large are the classes and/or other teaching groups? Small is generally better, though tiny sixth form groups may be taking staff away from younger classes.

5. How many teachers are there and how frequently do staff leave? High staff turnover is a bad sign.

6. If the school is co-educational, what does the school do to ensure that boys and girls have equal opportunities to perform well across the whole curriculum?

7. Are there special arrangements to help families whose first language is not English?

8. What is the school's policy to promote good race relations?

9. What arrangements are made to allow parents and staff to discuss progress?

10. What written reports, if any, are made to parents? Annual written reports will soon be compulsory.

11. What does the school do to keep parents in touch if there are problems, and are there any special facilities for pupils in difficulties with work or behaviour?

12. What part do parents play in the everyday life of the school?

13. Is there a PTA, a parents' room, and easy communication with parent-governors?

14. What activities are there for children out of school time?

15. Are there any plans for new buildings, or reorganisation which might affect the future of the school?

Judging standards

1. Is the children's work well presented and displayed around the school?

2. Are their books in good condition and is work well presented in them?

3. Is the work going on in classrooms disciplined and well-ordered?

This does not necessarily mean that the pupils will be sitting silently in rows. A great deal of class work these days involves discussion and practical work, but this should not degenerate into chaos.

4. How well looked after are the school premises? Even old buildings can be kept clean and pleasant. Is there evidence of graffiti on the walls and rubbish in the playgrounds? Are the toilets clean and undamaged?

5. Is the relationship between children and teachers relaxed and friendly or do the teachers seem tense and the children disorderly? Do any of the children look bored, or sulky or cowed?

6. Do staff appear to welcome parents as visitors and show confidence in explaining what they are doing?

7. Can staff explain clearly how they expect children to progress from year to year, and what arrangements they make for children who need special help at one time or another?

8. Is the school well-equipped for practical and creative subjects like design technology, information technology, home economics, business studies, art, music and science? Primary schools, as well as secondary schools, are expected to teach science and technology under the National Curriculum. Are computers in evidence and are they being used? Is there an adequate library and is that being used by children?

What if my child is bullied?

Schools can be terrifying for many children and bullying is a reality. Most schools have strong anti-bullying policies and you should immediately talk to the school if bullying occurs. Be sensitive and listen to your child's views on how to handle the situation. All children want to be liked and if possible sort out the problem by themselves.

How do I complain to a school?

All parents have a right to question the school on its methods, practices and standards. If you are dissatisfied you should write to or visit the school. Initially contact the form or year head, and if this does not prove satisfactory, then contact the head. Most schools have active Parent/Teacher Associations which are a useful source of support. You have the right to elect parent-governors to represent your views, and you can contact a parent-governor to ask them to take up your issue if you wish.

ORGANISING AFTER-SCHOOL CHILDCARE

Childcare is often more difficult to organise for children of school age than for the under-fives. There aren't many jobs around where you can arrive at 9.30 am after dropping the children off at school, leave at 2.45pm to take them home, and also not work during the school holidays and half-terms.

Kids clubs have been developed for this reason. They often provide a safe place to play before school and for two to three hours afterwards. They bridge the gap between school and working hours. There are over 1,500 clubs in the UK and there are plans to increase this to 3,000 with support from the government.

They are usually based in schools and use these facilities. Often the clubs pick up the children, and you only have to collect from the club when you've finished work or college.

Kids Clubs Network is the national umbrella body for holiday playschemes and out-of-school play and care for children aged 5–12.

GETTING SUPPORT AND ADVICE

It is important to explore all the options as sometimes your first and immediate choice cannot always suit your needs, and there could be much better alternatives around the corner.

Although childcare can be limited in some areas and with long waiting lists, many childcare organisations give priority to working lone parents. The best source of local childcare information is the **Childcare Division (Under Eights Department)** of your local Social Services, usually listed under the name of your local authority. The **Citizens Advice Bureau** and the **library** should also have information.

Contact the **local education authority** for school lists.

DISCUSSION POINTS

1. Use the childcare guide and tick the sources of childcare that could meet your needs.

2. Take the step-by-step guide and check out local childcare.

3. Use the school questions lists and see how your child's school meets your and your child's needs.

12
Enjoying your Children

Having children is often seen as a burden. They take your time and money, and one day they will leave you. This is the typical grumpy dad syndrome, but even grumpy dads smile occasionally, and if you let them your children can make you smile a lot of the time. It is not easy to see above the day-to-day survival of raising a family, but you must never lose sight of the principle that your children bring and will bring you much joy. Just stand back and observe them, see how they act and play. Most parents usually raise a smile when they see their kids fast asleep, curled up with teddy.

Case study: Martin loves his children
'Bringing up my children on my own means I don't have very much time alone and time to relax. The other day I was slumped in the chair, the kids were watching television, one was at the table doing his homework. I felt very much alone, and then I realised I wasn't as there were three people in this room who deeply loved me, they were my mates as well as my kids. It is amazing but when you do smile and look generally happy, the atmosphere around you is great. You laugh, the kids laugh. Being a parent is fun and should be about fun.'

GOING OUT WITH YOUR KIDS

We all like trips out and children especially, but going out doesn't have to mean going to a theme park or burgerbar. Going out could mean a walk to the shops, a nature trail in the local woods, a family cycling trip to the local park, feeding the ducks, visiting the local library, or going swimming. The importance of going out is the fun of doing something together, sharing, learning and laughing together.

Ideas for going out, places and things to do

Playing football	Watching football	Swimming
Theatre	Cinema	A walk in the park
Pond dipping		Picking strawberries

Visiting a stately home and grounds

Climbing a local hill		Nature trail in a local wood
Going to the local library	Seaside	Collecting wildflowers

BUILDING YOUR CONFIDENCE AS A FATHER

Being a dad is not easy and often we feel on the sidelines of the family, but being a father is very important. Perhaps the title of 'head of the household' has evolved to 'joint head', or perhaps you are a divorced dad and therefore the 'alternative head'. Whatever your situation, you should never underestimate the importance of your role as a father. Confidence is about feeling OK with yourself, and learning to be proud or what you have done and are achieving. To achieve better confidence, you need to:

- respect yourself

- take responsibility for yourself – for what you think, feel and do

- not see yourself purely in the role of father, but as a person in your own right

- ask for what you want – don't expect other people to guess what you want

- respect other people and their rights.

ARRANGING BABYSITTERS

Finding a babysitter and being able to pay them is the real nightmare of all parents. It is a question of relying on word of mouth amongst friends, putting ads in shop windows, contacting local parent clubs, asking at your child's playgroup. Babysitting circles are a good idea.

Think about letting the kids sleep over at a friend's house. Don't put obstacles in your way. Arranging a good source of evening childcare is essential if you want to **Go Out!**

KEEPING YOUR RELATIONSHIP HEALTHY

Children have two parents, and although they can be brought up very happily with one, the ideal for them is to have two happy and loving parents. This is not easy and relationships fail for a variety of reasons: financial, falling in love with someone else, violence, or just simply falling out of love. Whatever the reasons, your children are innocent bystanders, and preventive medicine is always the best solution. So if you are lucky and have a good relationship with the mother of your children, then keep it alive and healthy. Don't get bogged down in work and domestic childcare or let your partner do the same. Find time to relax and enjoy each other's company. The key is to talk, which is not easy for many men.

INTRODUCING YOUR CHILDREN TO YOUR NEW PARTNER

It is hoped that you are not in this situation, but as said before relationships do fail, and you will form new ones. Or you may have lost your partner through death. It is therefore highly likely if you are separated, divorced or widowed, that you will one day have to introduce your children to a new partner.

- Remember both your new partner and your children are independent beings and you cannot force them to like each other.

- Allow plenty of time on all sides.

- Stick to short initial meetings if possible, so that both sides get to know each other.

GOING ON HOLIDAY

It is appropriate as this book is coming to an end, and when the author at least is looking forward to a rest, to remind you that holidays are important both for you and for your children. Time spent together and having fun are the main ingredients. A holiday at home can be just as exciting as an exotic one overseas. You really don't have to spend a fortune in order to have a good time. Talk to your children about the sort of things they would like to do. Balance your needs with theirs.

Personal Action Plan Chart

Date

Name

What I want to do with the children

What I want to do with my partner

What I want to do with myself

Action to be taken

Problems (what might stop me from taking these actions)

Solutions

When? (time scale)

Comments

WRITING A PERSONAL FATHER ACTION PLAN

A personal action plan will help you to:

- focus on what you want for your future
- decide what action you need to take to achieve what you want
- think about the problems that you will need to resolve
- think about possible solutions to these problems
- plan in a way which will enable you to tackle problems and achieve what you want.

Include in your plan five goals that involve your children and your partner.

Use the chart on page 106 as a guide.

LEARNING TO BE PROUD OF WHAT YOU ARE ACHIEVING

You are doing a great job bringing up your children and you should be very proud of yourself. Being a parent is not easy. Being a father is hard.

The key to being a 'successful parent' is learning to be happy with yourself and think positively, even when you are facing a disaster. You have to believe that whatever you are facing, positive action can win the day.

There is no magical wand to wave, and life will be hard. No easy solutions, but you can slowly step by step improve your situation and achieve your goals. It may take time, but they are achievable. Remember, you have special people rooting for you, they are called your children.

DISCUSSION POINTS

1. Write your action plan and set five goals which you wish to achieve over the next year, with your partner and your children.

2. Discuss things that you enjoy doing with your children and things they enjoy doing with you, and plan a series of activities and trips.

3. Visit your local parent support group or perhaps establish one.

Glossary

Absent parent. A term introduced by the Child Support Act 1991. It refers to the parent who does not have the day-to-day care of the child, as opposed to the **parent with care**.

Access. New word for contact, used in Children Act 1989.

Adultery. Legal terms used to describe sexual intercourse by a husband or wife with a third party (of the opposite sex) at any time before a **decree absolute** of divorce. You could have been separated from your married partner for some time, and yet technically commit adultery, even though in your eyes the marriage is over. In law it is only over when a decree absolute is given by the courts.

Affidavit. A statement whose contents are sworn to be true. Used in legal procedures as a way of you substantiating your claims or in answer to another's claims against you.

Ante-natal. Ante means before, and natal means birth. Therefore before birth.

Au pair. Usually a young girl (18–25) learning language in a foreign country, providing **childcare** in return for accommodation, food and a small allowance.

Benefits. Financial assistance provided by the government whether through the Department of Social Security/Benefits Agency (income support, family credit, etc.) or through your local authority (housing and council tax benefit).

Bereavement. The state and sense of loss of a loved one.

Carer. A person who looks after the day-to-day welfare of others. A parent is a carer of his or her children.

Childcare. Care and oversight of a child. Usually refers to the arrangements for a child other than being cared for by parents or school. An additional service provided by other family members, friends, childminders, nannies, au pairs, playgroups, after-school clubs and nurseries.

Child Support Agency (CSA). The national body that deals with seeking **maintenance** from the absent parent. Part of the Department of Social Security.

Cohabitation. A couple living together as husband and wife but without being legally married.

Conciliation. Service provided by a number of organisations to mediate between couples on matters which arise during separation and divorce. Some conciliation schemes are run in association with the courts and some are run by voluntary organisations (See also **mediation**).

Contact. A contact order is one which enables a child literally to have some contact with the person in the order (usually the absent parent). Such contact could include visiting, staying overnight, sending and receiving letters, and so on.

Counselling. Service offered by a number of organisations, such as Relate, to anyone experiencing difficulties. Counsellors do not seek to give you the answers to your problems but to enable you to find the answers yourself through full and open discussion.

Creditors. People or organisations that you owe money to. Could include shops, banks, building societies, electricity board, etc.

Custody. Traditional term used to describe which parent had the fully responsibility for the child/children. The Children Act 1989 has changed towards giving every parent **parent responsibility** and in legal terms the word 'custody' has been replaced.

Debt. Money that you owe.

Decree absolute. Order dissolving a marriage.

Decree nisi. Document issued once the court is satisfied that the grounds for divorce are established, allowing a **petititioner** to apply to have the **decree** made **absolute** after a further six weeks and one day.

Embryo. After a woman's egg is fertilised by the male's sperm, it forms into an embryo which grows into a baby.

Endocrine glands. Produce hormones which circulate in the blood stream controlling the way the body works.

Ex-partner. Partner is a common term used for husband or wife, whether married or unmarried, but generally used when people are not married. Ex refers to former partner, husband or wife.

Gay parenting. Term used to describe a parent who has had children normally through intercourse with the opposite sex, but whose sexual orientation means they wish to have a relationship only with their own sex. Being gay does not impede in any way on their skills as a parent.

Infidelity. When a lover or partner is unfaithful by having sexual intercourse with another.

Maintenance. Payments made to an **ex-partner**, usually to help towards the living costs of that person and/or the children of the couple.

Mediation. Refers to the method of getting couples to discuss a full range of issues which arise as a result of separation and divorce. Includes discussion of arrangements for the children, financial and property matters. Has a broader focus than conciliation but basically means the same.

Parental responsibility. A term introduced by the Children Act 1989. Refers to the rights, duties, powers, responsibilities and authority which a parent has in relation to a child. Mothers and married fathers have this responsibility automatically. Other people, including unmarried fathers, can also acquire it through the courts.

Parent with care. A term introduced by the Child Support Act 1991. Refers to the parent who has the day-to-day care of the child, as opposed to the **absent parent**.

Partner. Term used to describe a live-in lover, husband, wife. Used in preference in this book and others as it covers relationships both within and outside marriage.

Petitioner. The **spouse** (husband or wife) who starts divorce proceedings by making a petition for divorce.

Prejudice. In the context of this book prejudice means an opinion or view made without proper study of the facts that gives an unfair judgement.

Reconciliation. Not to be confused with **conciliation**. Conciliation seeks to mediate between a couple in dispute. Reconciliation seeks to bring a couple together again.

Residence order. Used by Children Act 1989 to determine which parent the child/children lives with.

Respondent. Opposite to **Petititioner** in a divorce case.

Separation. Usual term to describe the period when a married couple decide to live apart prior to instigating divorce proceedings.

Shared parenting. Term used to describe a family situation where two parents live apart but the children spend substantial time with each parent on a regular basis. Both parents actively discuss the well-being of their children and make joint decisions.

Special needs. The wide range of disabilities and disadvantages that any individual, whether an adult or child, can suffer. Anything from dyslexia to Down's Syndrome.

Splitting up. Common term for a relationship/marriage ending.

Spouse. The husband or wife in a marriage.

Statutory charge. The power a statutory authority (government body) can place on your property in order to regain money you owe after it is sold.

Stress. Term used to describe a situation when you find great difficulty with coping. A state that everyone experiences and that causes confusion and anxiety which can lead to illness (physical and mental). Relaxation and talking to others about your problems are the recommended way to tackle stress.

Uterus. The womb of a woman – the place where the baby develops. The wall of the uterus is made of muscle and enlarges during pregnancy as the baby grows.

Will. A document that states how you want your belongings and assets distributed amongst your family and friends, or others such as charities, in the event of your death. A lone parent would also nominate who would be the guardian and carer of their children and how they wish their children to be cared for. Usually one or more persons are nominated as executors of the will. These executors are people you know and trust to carry out your wishes.

Useful Addresses

PARTICULAR USEFULNESS TO FATHERS

Parentline. National organisation with a network of local telephone helplines run by trained parent volunteers. Supports parents who need help or are finding it difficult to cope. Details can be found in the local telephone directory or by contacting (01449) 677707.

Parent Network, 44-46 Caversham Road, London NW5 2DS. Tel: (0171) 485 8535. Parent Network has a Parent-Link programme which offers a range of services for parents of children of all ages. Contact the London office to find out your local contact.

Families Need Fathers. Tel: (0171) 613 5060. Mainly concerned with helping children to maintain relationships with both parents following divorce or separation. Also advise and support parents and have a national network of voluntary contacts.

Family Rights Group, The Print House, 18 Ashwin Street, London E8 3DL. Tel: (0171) 249 0008. Gives practical and legal advice to families, particularly for parents with children who may go into or are in local authority care.

Family Planning Association, 27 Mortimer Street, London W1N 7RJ. Tel: (0171) 636 7866.

National Childbirth Trust, Alexandra House, Oldham Terrace, Acton, London W3 6NH. Tel: (0181) 992 8637.

GENERAL ADVICE

Citizens Advice Bureaux (CABs), 115–123 Pentonville Road, London N1 9LZ. Tel: (0171) 833 2181. Details of your CABs can be found in the telephone directory or by phoning the national office. CABs can help with a wide range of problems and may hold legal sessions and provide debt counselling.

Federation of Independent Advice Centres (FIAC), 13 Stockwell Road, London SW9 9AU. Tel: (0171) 274 1893. A network of advice centres around the country.

BENEFITS

Child Benefit and One Parent Benefit
Child Benefit Centre, DSS Washington, Newcastle-Upon-Tyne NE88 1AA.

General Benefit information
The Child Poverty Action Group, 1–5 Bath Street, London EC1V 9PY. Tel: (0171) 253 3406. Produces a range of material including *The National Welfare Benefits Handbook*.

BEREAVEMENT

Cruse Bereavement Care, Cruse house, 26 Sheen Road, Richmond TW9 1UR. Tel: (0181) 940 4818. Helpline: (0181) 322 7227 (9.30 am – 5 pm Mon–Fri). Has support groups around the country for the bereaved.

Bereavement Trust, Stanford Hall, Loughborough, Leicestershire LE12 5QR. Tel: (01509) 852333. Provides information about bereavement support services across the country.

Foundation for Black Bereaved Families, 11 Kingston Square, Salters Hill, London SE19 1JE. Tel: (0181) 661 7228. Provides support and advice to bereaved black families across the country.

The Gay Bereavement Project, c/o Gay Switchboard. Tel: (0171) 837 7324 (24 hours). Based in London, but can offer contacts for other parts of the country.

Institute of Family Therapy, 43 New Cavendish Street, London W1M 7RG. The Elizabeth Raven Memorial Fund offers free counselling to newly bereaved families or those with terminally ill family members.

National Association of Bereaved Services, 668 Charlton Street, London NW11 1JR. Tel: (0181) 388 2153. Provides a national network of support groups for the bereaved and can put you in touch with services in your area.

CHILDCARE

Kids Club Network, 279–281 Whitechapel Road, London E1 1BY. Tel: (0171) 247 3009. Gives advice and information on all aspects of out-of-school childcare. KCN is the national umbrella body for holiday playschemes and out-of-school play and care for children aged five to twelve.

The Parent Helpline. Tel: (0171) 837 5513 (10 am – 5 pm). National helpline which gives parents details of childcare in their area.

Daycare Trust/National Childcare Campaign, Wesley House, 4 Wild Court, London WC2B 4AU. Tel: (0171) 405 5617.

National Childminding Association, 8 Mason Hill, Bromley, Kent BR2 9EY. Tel: (0181) 464 6164.

The National Early Years Network, 77 Holloway Road, London N7 8JZ. Tel: (0171) 607 9573. Provides details of local under-eight services.

National Association of Toy and Leisure Libraries, 68 Churchway, London NW1 1LT. Provides information on local toy libraries.

Pre-School Learning Alliance, 61/63 Kings Cross Road, London WC1X 9LL. Tel: (0171) 833 0991. Umbrella organisation for all the voluntary-run playgroups in the UK.

CHILDREN

Childline, Freepost 1111, London N1 0BR. Tel: 0800 1111. Free counselling service for children. Available 24 hours a day.

National Children's Bureau, 8 Wakeley Street, London EC1V 7QE. Tel: (0171) 843 6000.

Cry-sis, BM Cry-sis, London WC1N 3XX. Tel: (0171) 404 5011. Self-help and support for families with excessively crying, sleepless and demanding children.

NSPCC (National Society for the Prevention of Cruelty to Children), 42 Curton Road, London CC2A 3NH. Tel: (0171) 825 2500. Can be contacted for information and advice relating to the welfare of children.

COUNSELLING

Your GP may be able of offer counselling or refer you for counselling.

Relate–Marriage Guidance, Herbert Gray College, Little Church Street, Rugby, Warwickshire CV21 3AP. Has local branches around the country. Can be used by married or unmarried couples.

Samaritans. For details of local groups see the telephone directory or Tel: (01753) 532713.

British Association for Counselling, 1 Regent Place, Rugby, Warwickshire CV21 2PJ. Tel: (01788) 578328.

DEBT

CABs (details on page 112).
National Debtline, 318 Summer Lane, Birmingham B19 3RL. Tel: (0121) 359 8501. Offers specialist debt advice and support.
Creditcure Voluntary Association, 109 Bramford Road, Ipswich, Suffolk IP1 2PL. Produces a newsletter and a debt survival manual. Send SAE.

DISABILITY/SPECIAL NEEDS

Citizen Advocacy Information and Training (CAIT), Unit 2K, Leroy House, 436 Essex Road, London N1 3QP. Tel: (0171) 359 8289. Information about advocacy services which help people with disabilities to deal with officials.
Contact-a-family, 70 Tottenham Court Road, London W1PP 0HA. Helpline: (0171) 383 3555. National charity providing information and support for parents of children with special needs.
Disability Alliance (ERA), 1st Floor East, Universal House, 88–94 Wentworth Street, London E1 7SA. Tel: (0171) 247 8776. Provides information and advice by telephone and letter to people with disabilities and their carers.
Parentability, c/o National Childbirth Trust, Alexandra House, Oldham Terrace, London W3 6NH. Provides advice and has details of support groups and resources for parents with disabilities.

EDUCATION

The National Confederation of Parent–Teacher Associations, 43 Stonebridge Road, Northfleet, Gravesend, Kent DD11 9DS. Offers advice on organising parents groups in schools. Advice on parents' rights.

EMPLOYMENT

Parents at Work, 77 Holloway Road, London N7 8JZ. Tel: (0171) 700 0281. Provides information on working parent support groups in the UK and all aspects of working combined with caring for children.

New Ways to work, 309 Upper Street, London N1 2TY. Tel: (0171) 226 4026. Publishes booklets and fact sheets on all aspects of job sharing. Enquiries: Tuesdays (10 am – 1 pm) Wednesday (12 noon – 3 pm).

Ownbase, 68 First Avenue, Bush Hill Park, Enfield, Middlesex EN1 1BN. A national network and newsletter for people who work from home.

FAMILY

National Stepfamily Association, 72 Willesden Lane, London NW6 7TA. Tel: (0171) 372 0844 (office). (0171) 372 0846 (counselling). Provides advice, support and information to stepfamiles; confidential telephone counselling service, newsletters and local support groups.

The Family Welfare Association, 501–505 Kingsland Road, London E8 4AU. Tel: (0171) 254 6251. Provides social work and social care services to families and individuals. FWA offers a variety of services to people facing social and emotional difficulties, including family and relationship problems, bereavement, loneliness, poverty, unemployment and homelessness.

GAY

Lesbian and Gay Switchboard, Tel: (0171) 837 7324. Can provide details of local lesbian and gay support groups and switchboards.

HEALTH

Health Information Service. Tel: 0800 665544. Free confidential information service dealing with individual health enquiries offering facts and advice on health services in your region.

MIND (National Association for Mental Health), Granta House, 15–19 Broadway, Stratford, London E15 4BQ. Tel: (0181) 519 2122. Provides information about a range of health problems and has leaflets about treatment and therapies. Also gives legal advice. Local MIND groups offer different services such as drop-in centres, counselling, referral to counsellors.

LEGAL

Children's Legal Centre, c/o University of Essex, Winehoe Park, Colchester CO4 3SQ. Tel: (01206) 872562. Advice Line: (01206) 873820 (2–5 pm Mon–Fri). Provides advice on young people and the law.

Disability Law Service, 116 Princeton Street, London WC1R 4BB. Tel: (0171) 831 8031/7740. A free service for people with disabilities and their families, providing advice and some representation on all aspects of the law.

Gay and Lesbian Legal Advice (GLAD), Tel: (0171) 253 2043. A free phone line open in the evenings, providing free legal advice and referral to solicitors.

Law Centre's Federation, Duchess House, 18–19 Warren Street, London W1P 5DB. Tel: (0171) 387 8570. Will give you details of your local law centre which can offer free legal advice and representation on specific issues.

Legal Aid Head Office, 85 Grays Inn Road, London WC1X 8AA. Tel: (0171) 813 1000.

Solicitors Family Law Association (SFLA), PO Box 302, Orpington, Kent BR6 8QX. Tel: (01689) 850227. An association of solicitors specialising in family law. Send a stamped addressed envelope for a list of local solicitor members.

LONE PARENT ORGANISATIONS/GROUPS

Gingerbread, 16–17 Clerkenwell Close, London EC1R 0AA. Tel: (0171) 336 8183. Advice Line: (0171) 336 8184. The nationally recognised self-help association for one parent families. There are about 400 local groups operating in the UK and they meet regularly to provide mutual support and help for members and their children. Many groups also run a range of social activities.

Gingerbread Northern Ireland, 169 University Street, Belfast BT7 1HR. Tel: (01232) 231147.

Gingerbread Scotland, Maryhill Community Hall, 304 Maryhill Road, Glasgow G20 7YE. Tel: (0141) 353 0989.

Gingerbread Wales, 16 Albion Chambers, Cambrian Place, Swansea SA1 1RN. Tel: (01792) 648728.

National Council for One Parent Families, 255 Kentish Town Road, London NW5 2LX. Tel: (0171) 267 1361. Offers information for lone parents on welfare benefits, housing, divorce, maintenance, legal matters and bereavement.

Single Parent Action Network (SPAN), Millpond, Lower Ashley Road, Easton, Bristol BS5 0YJ. Tel: (0117) 951 4231. A nationwide network of self-help organisations for single parents; particularly concerned with poverty, racism and women's issues and can help new groups.

Scottish Council for Single Parents, 13 Gayfield Square, Edinburgh EH1 3AX. Tel: (0131) 556 3899.

One Plus, 39 Hope Street, Glasgow G2 6AF. Tel: (0141) 221 7150. Advice and information for lone parents in Scotland.

Single parent fathers

All the above groups include single parent dads. However, there are groups around the UK that cater for the particular needs of fathers bringing up their children alone.

Single Dads Support, 3 Oregon Close, New Malden, Surrey. Send SAE for information.

Fatherhood Support Group, The Old Library, New Street, Dawley, Telford, Shropshire. Tel: (01952) 501272.

MAINTENANCE

Child Support Agency, Millbank Tower, 21–24 Millbank, London SW1 4QU. Public Enquiry Line: (0345) 133133. General advice on any aspect of child maintenance.

MEDIATION

National Family Mediation Service (NFM), Charitybase, The Chandlery, 50 Westminster Bridge Road, London SE1 7QY. Tel: (0171) 721 7658. Can put you in touch with a local service, where you can receive mediation help. Some charge a fee for mediation sessions, while others are free. You may get help with fees under the Legal Aid scheme.

Family and Divorce Centre, 162 Tennison Road, Cambridge CB1 2DP. Tel: (01223) 460136. Provide a range of services from legal advice to mediation and conciliation for people seeking divorce.

Family Mediators Association, The Old House, Rectory Gardens, Henbury, Bristol BS10 7AQ. Tel: (0117) 950 0140.

Family Mediation (Northern Ireland), 76 Dublin Road, Belfast BT2 7HP. Tel: (01232) 322914.

Family Mediation (Scotland), 127 Rose Street, South Lane,

Edinburgh EH2 5BB. Tel: (0131) 220 1610.

Family Mediation (Wales), 33 Westgate Street, Cardiff, South Glamorgan CF1 1JE. Tel: (01222) 229692.

National Family Mediation, 9 Tavistock Place, London WC1H 9SN. Tel: (0171) 383 5993. Has details of mediation services around the country.

Divorce Conciliation and Advisory Service (DCAS), 38 Ebury Street, London SW1W OLU. Tel: (0171) 730 2422.

PARENTING

Exploring Parenthood, Latimer Educational Centre, 194 Freston Road, London W10 6TT. Tel: (0181) 960 1678. A free national telephone advice line providing advice and counselling for parents. Also runs the Moyenda Project for black and Asian parents.

Home-Start, Head Office, 2 Salisbury Road, Leicester LE1 7QR. Tel: (0116) 255 4988. Has local schemes which offer regular support, friendship and practical help to families with at least one child under five. Volunteers visit families in their own homes. Details of local groups can be found in the local telephone directory or by contacting the head office.

Step-family, 72 Willesden Lane, London NW6 7TA. Tel: (0171) 372 0844; (0171) 372 0846 (counselling).

Parents Anonymous. Tel: (0171) 263 8918 or (0181) 689 3136. A telephone helpline for all parents under stress.

Twin and Multiple Birth Association, 54 Parkway, Exeter, Devon EX2 9NF. Tel: (01392) 431605.

Association of Shared Parenting, PO Box 2000, Dudley, West Midlands DY1 1Y2. Promotes the child's right to the nurture of both parents after separation or divorce. Encourages and supports parents in fulfilment of this right.

PREGNANCY ADVICE AND COUNSELLING

British Pregnancy Advisory Service (BPAS), Austy Manor, Wooton Waven, Solihull, West Midlands B95 6BX.

Brook Advisory Centres, 153a East Street, London SE17 2SD. Tel: (0171) 240 0953.

RELATIONSHIPS

Relate, Herbert Grey College, Little Church Street, Rugby, Warwickshire CV21 3AP. Tel: (01788) 73241. Confidential counselling on relationship problems of any kind.

Marriage Guidance (Scotland), 105 Hanover Street, Edinburgh EH2 1DG. Tel: (0131) 225 5006.

National Council for the Divorced and Separated, 13 High Street, Little Shelford, Cambridge CB2 5ES. Tel: (0116) 270595. Offers advice and the chance to meet others who are or have been through similar experiences.

Divorces Conciliation and Advisory Service, 38 Ebury Street, London SW1W OLU. Tel: (0171) 730 2422. Help and advice for parents to maintain workable arrangements of joint care for their children.

Both Parents Forever, 39 Cloonmore Avenue, Orpington, Kent BR6 9LE. Tel: (01689) 854343. Promotes the rights of grandparents, parents and children. Helps trace and return children in child abduction cases.

Catholic Marriage Advisory Council, Clitherow House, 1 Blythe Mew, Blythe Road, London W14 ONW. Tel: (0171) 371 1341.

Further Reading

FATHER ISSUES

Goodies and Daddies: A–Z Guide to Fatherhood, Michael Rosen (John Murray). An essential read and a very funny one.
Fathering for Men, Martin Francis (Generation Books, 1986).
Fatherhood: Men Write about Fathering (Virago 1992).
The Role of the Father in Child Development (John Wray, New York 1981).
Reassessing Fatherhood: New Observations on Fathers and the Modern Family, Charlie Lewis and Margaret O'Brien (Sage 1987).
The Uncertain Father: Exploring Modern Fatherhood (Gateway Books 1987).
Father over Forty – Becoming an Older Father, Jeremy Hayward (Optima).
Fatherhood, Brian Jackson (Allen & Unwin 1983).

BABIES

Twins Handbook, Elizabeth Friedrich and Cherry Rowland (Robinson Paperback). Covers prebirth to first schooldays.
Baby Care Book: A Practical Guide to the First Three Years, Dr Miriam Stoppard (Dorling Kindersley).
The Good Deal Directory Guide to Bringing Up Baby on a Budget, Noelle Walsh (Pan). Good guide on where to go for baby bargains.

BABIES AND DADS

How to be a Pregnant Father, Peter Mayle (1980).
The Baby Book for Dads (New English Library 1980).
Expectant Father, Betty Parsons (Elliot Right Way Books 1984).

BENEFITS

National Welfare Benefits Handbook & rights Guide to Non Means Tested Benefits Child Poverty Action Group (CPAG).
How to Claim State Benefits, Martin Rathfelder (How To Books).

BEREAVEMENT

Bereavement, Christopher Golding (Crowood Press 1991). The practical aspects of bereavement.
Dealing with a Death in the Family, Sylvia Murphy (How To Books 1997).
Which? Consumer Guides – What to Do When Someone Dies, Paul Harris (Which? Books, distributed by Penguin Group). How to deal with the practical arrangements that have to be made after death.

CHILDCARE

Free to Work – Comprehensive Guide to Childcare in England and Wales, Gingerbread.
What's on Where? The National Guide to School Age Childcare, Kids Club Network.

CHILDREN AND ISSUES

Helping Children Cope with Divorce, Rosemary Wells, (Sheldon Press).
Helping Children Cope with Grief, Rosemary Wells (Sheldon Press).
Facing Grief – Bereavement and the Young Adult, Susan Wallbank (Lutterworth Press 1991). One of the few books around written specifically for young people, this has particularly good sections on the different effects of a mother's or father's death.

CHILDREN'S BOOKS ON DADS

Sam's New Dad, Nigel Snell (Hamish Hamilton).
My Dad Takes Care of Me, Patrician Quinlan (Annick Press).

CHILDREN'S BOOKS ON FAMILY CHANGES

The following are children's books that tackle issues of family break-up, divorce, bereavement and living in single parent families.

Children Don't Divorce, Rosemary Stones (Dinosaur Talk It Over Series).
You Can be Spurs, Chris Ashley (Walker).
Mike's Lonely Summer, Caroline Nystrom (Lion).
Dad And Me series (Walker).
Finish the Story, Dad, Nicola Smee (Walker).
Emma's Monster, Marjorie Darke (Walker).
Crazy Christmas, Jeanne Bettancourt (Pan Macmillan).
The Haunted Sand, Hugh Scott (Walker).
Worlds Apart, Jill Murphy (Walker).
Anna Magdalena – The Little Girl with the Big Name (Lion).
Grief in Children, Atle Dyregov (Jessica Kingsley 1990).
How it Feels When a Parent Dies, edited by J. Krementz (Gollancz 1986). Accounts by eighteen children of different ages of how they experienced a parent's death.
I Never Told Her I Loved Her, Sandra Chick (Livewire Books 1989). A novel about a teenager coping with her mother's death and her new role as 'woman of the house'.
The Secret Garden, Frances Hodgson Burnett (Puffin 1911). Classic children's book about two bereaved children finding friendship and renewed faith in life.

CUSTODY

Arrangements for children in the family (NCOPF).

DEBT

Debt Advice Handbook, Mike Woolfe and Jill Mason (CPAG).
Debt – A Survival Guide (Office of Fair Trading).

DIVORCE/RELATIONSHIP BREAK-UP

Dad's Place – A Guide for Fathers After Divorce, Jill Burnett (Harrap Collins).
Being There: Fathers After Divorce (Relate Centre for Family Studies).
Men and Divorce, John Abulafia (Fontana). This is the first book to look at the emotional side of the divorce trauma from the man's point of view.
The Relate Guide to Starting Again, Sarah Litvinoff (Vermillion). A guide to the emotional aspects of dealing with a separation and

how to help your children.

Divorced Parenting Dr Soc (Goldstein).

The Which? Guide to Divorce, Helen Garlick.

Going it Alone – Two Guides for Married and Unmarried Women (SHAC. Tel: (0171) 404 6929).

How to Survive Divorce, Roy Van de Brink-Budgen (How To Books).

FAMILY

Families and How to Survive Them, Robin Skynner and John Cleese (Mandarin Paperbacks 1990). An invaluable read for anyone wanting to understand how relationships within families have implications for the rest of your life.

HEALTH

Which? Guide to Men's Health, Dr Steve Carroll (Penguin). Good guide and a very good chapter on fatherhood.

HOLIDAYS

Holidays for One Parent Families (National Council for One Parent Families).

The Parent Guide – Children's Holidays (Kupperand).

LAW

When Parents Separate – a Handbook of Law and Practice (Children's Legal Centre).

MAINTENANCE

A Guide to Child Support Maintenance (Child Support Agency).

Maintenance and the Child Support Agency (NCOPF).

For Parents who Live Apart (Child Support Agency).

SINGLE PARENT ISSUES

Successful Single Parenting, Mike Lilley (How To Books).

The Single Parents Survival Guide – How to Go It Alone Successfully, Caroline Buchanan and Sandra Sedgbeer.

One Parent Families, Sue Watkins (Crowood Press).

One Parent Plus – A Handbook for Single Parents, Jane Ward (Optima).

Just Me and the Kids – A Manual for Lone Parents (Gingerbread/ Bedford Square Press).

Soul Providers, edited by Gil McNeil (Virago). Eighteen lone parents give their personal view of life as a single parent.

Single and Pregnant (NCOPF).

How to Help: a Guide for Family and Friends of Lone Parents (NCOPF).

SPECIAL NEEDS

Your Child with Special Needs, Susan Kerr (Hodder & Stoughton). A good parents guide to all you need to know about caring for a child with special needs.

STEPFAMILIES

Understanding Stepfamilies (National Stepfamily Association).

Diary of a Stepfather, Leslie Wilson (National Stepfamily Association).

Index